It's another Quality Book from CGP

This book is for anyone doing Edexcel Modular
GCSE Mathematics at Foundation Level.

Whatever subject you're doing it's the same
old story — there are lots of facts and you've just got
to learn them. KS4 Maths is no different.

Happily this CGP book gives you all that important
information as clearly and concisely as possible.

It's also got some daft bits in to try and make the whole
experience at least vaguely entertaining for you.

What CGP is all about

Our sole aim here at CGP is to produce the highest quality
books — carefully written, immaculately presented and
dangerously close to being funny.

Then we work our socks off to get them out to you
— at the cheapest possible prices.

Contents

Calculating Tips 2

Unit 1 — Statistics and Probability

Fractions, Decimals and Percentages 4
Percentages 5
Ratio 6
Best Buys 8
Probability 9
Probability — Relative Frequency 11
Data 12
Mean, Median, Mode and Range 15
Frequency Tables 16
Averages and Grouped Data 17
Tables, Charts and Graphs 19
Scatter Graphs 21
Bar Charts and Comparing Data 22
Pie Charts 23
Revision Summary for Unit 1 — Part 1 24
Negative Numbers and Letters 25
X and Y Coordinates 26
Straight-Line Graphs 27
Straight-Line Graphs — Gradients 28
Real-life Graphs 29
Rounding Off 31
Accuracy and Estimating 33
Conversion Factors and Metric Units 34
Drawing and Measuring 36
Clock Time Questions 38
Revision Summary for Unit 1 — Part 2 39

Unit 2 — Number, Algebra and Geometry 1

Ordering Numbers and Place Value 40
Multiplying by 10, 100, etc 41
Dividing by 10, 100, etc 42
Addition and Subtraction 43
Multiplying Without a Calculator 44
Dividing Without a Calculator 45
Prime Numbers 46
Multiples, Factors and Prime Factors 47
LCM and HCF 48
Powers 49
Square Roots and Cube Roots 50
Fractions 51
Fractions and Recurring Decimals 53
Algebra 54
Making Formulas from Words 56
Special Number Sequences 57

Number Patterns and Sequences 58
Midpoint of a Line Segment 60
Drawing Straight-Line Graphs 61
Straight-Line Graphs — $y = mx + c$ 62
More Graphs 63
Revision Summary for Unit 2 — Part 1 64
Angles 65
Angles — The Rules 66
Parallel Lines 67
2D Shapes 68
2D Shapes — Circles 69
3D Shapes and Similarity 70
Symmetry 71
Perimeters 72
Areas 73
Volume and Surface Area 75
Imperial Units 76
Speed 77
Revision Summary for Unit 2 — Part 2 78

Unit 3 — Number, Algebra and Geometry 2

More Percentages 79
Percentages and Reciprocals 80
Solving Equations 81
Trial and Improvement 83
Inequalities 84
Quadratic Graphs 85
Regular Polygons 86
Congruence and Tessellation 87
Pythagoras' Theorem 88
Solids and Nets 89
The Four Transformations 90
Enlargements 92
Combinations of Transformations 94
Revision Summary for Unit 3 — Part 1 95
Triangle Construction 96
Loci and Constructions 97
Circles — Area and Circumference 99
More Area and Volume 100
Maps and Scales 101
Compass Directions and Bearings 103
Revision Summary for Unit 3 — Part 2 104

Answers 105
Index 109

Published by Coordination Group Publications Ltd.

Written by Richard Parsons

Updated by: Rosie Gillham, Neil Hastings, Simon Little, Julie Wakeling, Janet West, Sarah Williams

Proofreading by: Sally Gill, Sharon Keeley

ISBN: 978 1 84762 090 3

Groovy website: www.cgpbooks.co.uk
Printed by Elanders Hindson Ltd, Newcastle upon Tyne.
Jolly bits of clipart from CorelDRAW®

Calculating Tips

Ah, the glorious world of GCSE Maths. OK — maybe it's more like wiffy socks at times, but learn it you must. Edexcel Modular Maths is split into 3 units, each with their own exam — yuk. Thankfully there are some nifty exam tricks you only have to learn once, which could get you marks in all 3 exams. Read on...

BODMAS

Brackets, Other, Division, Multiplication, Addition, Subtraction

BODMAS tells you the ORDER in which these operations should be done:
Work out Brackets first, then Other things like squaring, then Divide / Multiply groups of numbers before Adding or Subtracting them.

This set of rules works really well, so remember the word BODMAS.

Example: A mysterious quantity T, is given by: $T = (P - 7)^2 + 4R/Q$
Find the value of T when P = 4, Q = -2 and R = 3

Write down the formula: $T = (P - 7)^2 + 4R/Q$
Put the numbers in: $T = (4 - 7)^2 + 4 \times 3/\text{-}2$
Then work it out in stages : $= (-3)^2 + 4 \times 3/\text{-}2$
                               $= 9 + 4 \times 3/\text{-}2$
                               $= 9 + \text{-}6$
                               $= 9 - 6 = \underline{3}$

Note BODMAS in operation:
Brackets worked out first, then squared. Multiplications and divisions done before finally adding and subtracting.

Always Check Your Answer

It's always a good idea to check your answers by working backwards through your calculations.

That way you can pick up any silly mistakes you might have made.

Example: If $y = 2x^2 + 3$, find the value of y when x = 3.

Answer: $y = 2 \times (3)^2 + 3$ Check: $21 - 3 = 18$
         $= 2 \times 9 + 3$ $18 \div 2 = 9$
         $= 18 + 3$ $\sqrt{9} = 3$
         $= \underline{21}$

Hurray — you've got the same number you started with.

Don't Be Scared of Wordy Questions

About a third of the marks on your exam come from answering wordy, real-life questions. For these, you don't just have to do the maths, you've got to work out what the question's asking you to do. Relax and work through them step by step.

1) READ the question carefully. Work out what bit of maths you need to answer it.
2) Underline the INFORMATION YOU NEED to answer the question — you might not have to use all the numbers they give you.
3) Write out the question IN MATHS and answer it, showing all your working clearly.

Example: A return car journey from Carlisle to Manchester uses $\frac{4}{7}$ of a tank of petrol.
It costs £56 for a full tank of petrol.
How much does the journey cost?

1) The "$\frac{4}{7}$" tells you this is a fractions question.

It doesn't matter where they're driving from and to.

2) You need £56 (the cost of a full tank) and $\frac{4}{7}$ (the fraction of the tank used).

3) You want to know $\frac{4}{7}$ of £56, so in maths:
$$£56 \times \frac{4}{7} = \underline{£32}$$

Don't forget the units in your final answer — this is a question about cost in pounds, so the units will be £.

Fractions questions are covered on page 45.

Calculating Tips

You're allowed to use a calculator in the Unit 1 and 3 exams — hurray! Make sure you know how your shiny grey friend can help you, and watch the marks roll in. Here's just a few things you'll end up using all the time.

BODMAS and the BRACKETS BUTTONS (and)

1) This is really important when you want to work out even a simple thing like $\dfrac{23 + 45}{64 \times 3}$.

2) You can't just press 23 $+$ 45 $\div$ 64 $\times$ 3 $=$ — it will be <u>completely wrong</u>.

3) The calculator follows BODMAS, so it'll think you mean $23 + \dfrac{45}{64} \times 3$.

4) The secret is to <u>OVERRIDE</u> the automatic <u>BODMAS</u> order of operations using the <u>BRACKETS BUTTONS</u>. Anything in brackets is worked out before anything else happens to it.

5) So all you have to do is write a couple of <u>pairs of brackets</u> into the expression like this: $\dfrac{(23 + 45)}{(64 \times 3)}$

6) Then just type it <u>as it's written</u>: $($ 23 $+$ 45 $)$ $\div$ $($ 64 $\times$ 3 $)$ $=$

It's OK to have brackets within other brackets too, <u>e.g. $(4 + (5 \div 2))$</u>. As a rule, you can't cause trouble by putting too many brackets in... **SO LONG AS THEY ALWAYS GO IN PAIRS**.

The Fraction Button: $a\frac{b}{c}$

Use this <u>as much as possible</u> in the calculator papers. It's very easy and dead useful.

1) To enter $\frac{1}{4}$ press 1 $a\frac{b}{c}$ 4

2) To enter $1\frac{3}{5}$ press 1 $a\frac{b}{c}$ 3 $a\frac{b}{c}$ 5

3) To work out $\frac{1}{5} \times \frac{3}{4}$ press 1 $a\frac{b}{c}$ 5 $\times$ 3 $a\frac{b}{c}$ 4 $=$

4) To <u>reduce a fraction to its lowest terms</u> enter it and press $=$ e.g. $\frac{9}{12}$ — 9 $a\frac{b}{c}$ 12 $=$ $\boxed{3\rfloor4}$ $= \frac{3}{4}$

5) To convert between <u>mixed</u> and <u>top-heavy</u> fractions press SHIFT $a\frac{b}{c}$.
E.g. $2\frac{3}{8}$ — 2 $a\frac{b}{c}$ 3 $a\frac{b}{c}$ 8 $=$ SHIFT $a\frac{b}{c}$ which gives $\frac{19}{8}$

The MEMORY BUTTONS (STO Store, RCL Recall)

These are really useful for keeping a number you've just calculated, so you can use it again shortly afterwards.

E.g. Find $\dfrac{840}{15 + 12\sin40}$ — just work out the <u>bottom line</u> first and <u>stick it in the memory</u>.

So press 15 $+$ 12 SIN 40 $=$ and then STO M to keep the result of the bottom line in the memory. Then you simply press 840 $\div$ RCL M $=$, and the answer is 36.98.

> The memory buttons might work a bit differently on your calculator. Note, if your calculator has an '<u>Ans</u>' button, you can do the same thing — the Ans button gives you the result you got when you <u>last pressed</u> the '=' button.

Make Sure You Know What Your Answer Means

It's taken 2 minutes of frenzied button pressing and finally your calculator screen looks like this.
Before you merrily jot down 3.6 as your answer, think about <u>what it means</u> — 3.6 what? $\boxed{3.6}$
Pipers piping? It sounds silly, but it can lose you easy marks in the exam. E.g. If you're answering a money question, 3.6 won't get you any marks — you'll probably need to write £3.60.

Learn these two pages, store, then recall...

Learn this stuff — it can really help you rack up marks whichever exam you're doing. Right, on with the rest of the show. Laaaaaaaadies and gentlemeeeeeeen — I give you, the one, the only — Edexcel Maths G C S Eeee.

Fractions, Decimals and Percentages

The one word that could describe all these three is <u>PROPORTION</u>.

Fractions, decimals and percentages are simply <u>three different ways</u> of expressing a <u>proportion</u> of something — and it's pretty important you should see them as <u>closely related and completely</u> <u>interchangeable</u> with each other. This table shows the really common conversions which you should know straight off without having to work them out:

Fraction	Decimal	Percentage
1/2	0.5	50%
1/4	0.25	25%
3/4	0.75	75%
1/3	0.333333... or $0.\dot{3}$	$33\frac{1}{3}$%
2/3	0.666666.... or $0.\dot{6}$	$66\frac{2}{3}$%
1/10	0.1	10%
2/10	0.2	20%
X/10	0.X	X0%
1/5	0.2	20%
2/5	0.4	40%

⅓ and ⅔ have what're known as '<u>recurring</u>' decimals — the same pattern of numbers carries on <u>repeating</u> itself forever. (Except here, the pattern's just a single 3 or a single 6. You could have, for instance: 0.143143143...)

The more of those conversions you learn, the better — but for those that you <u>don't know</u>, you must <u>also learn</u> how to <u>convert</u> between the three types. These are the methods:

Fraction $\xrightarrow{\text{Divide (use your calculator if you can) e.g. } \frac{1}{2} \text{ is } 1 \div 2}$ Decimal $\xrightarrow{\times \text{ by 100} \quad \text{e.g. } 0.5 \times 100}$ Percentage
= 0.5   = 50%

Fraction $\xleftarrow{\text{The tricky one}}$ Decimal $\xleftarrow{\div \text{ by 100}}$ Percentage

<u>Converting decimals to fractions</u> is only possible for <u>exact decimals</u> that haven't been rounded off. It's simple enough, but it's best illustrated by examples — see below. You should be able to work out what the simple rule is.

$0.6 = \frac{6}{10}$ $0.3 = \frac{3}{10}$ $0.7 = \frac{7}{10}$ $0.x = \frac{x}{10}$ etc.

$0.12 = \frac{12}{100}$ $0.78 = \frac{78}{100}$ $0.45 = \frac{45}{100}$ $0.05 = \frac{5}{100}$ etc.

$0.345 = \frac{345}{1000}$ $0.908 = \frac{908}{1000}$ $0.024 = \frac{24}{1000}$ $0.xyz = \frac{xyz}{1000}$ etc.

These can then be <u>cancelled down</u>.

You can use your calculator to cancel down fractions — see p.3.

<u>Recurring</u> decimals like 0.3333... are all actually just <u>fractions</u> in disguise. But don't worry, this is covered more in Unit 2.

Oh, what's recurrin'?...

Knowing all of the <u>top table</u> and the <u>4 conversion processes</u> for FDP will speed you up nicely in exams.

1) Turn the following decimals into fractions and reduce to their simplest form.
   a) 0.6   b) 0.02   c) 0.77   d) 0.555   e) 5.6

Percentages

This page is all about <u>percentages</u> in real-life situations. It's a thinly-veiled attempt by examiners to make maths more 'relevant'. So let's humour them — it's bound to be in the exam.

Discounts, VAT, Interest, Increase, etc.

<u>MOST</u> percentage questions are like this: | Work out 'something %' of 'something else'.

E.g. "Find 20% of £60."

This is the method to use:

1) <u>WRITE IT DOWN:</u>   Find 20% of £60.

2) <u>TRANSLATE INTO MATHS:</u> $\frac{20}{100} \times 60$

3) <u>WORK IT OUT:</u>   20 ÷ 100 × 60 = <u>£12</u>

Two Important Details:

Make sure you remember them!

1) <u>'Per cent' means 'out of 100'</u>

so <u>20%</u> means '20 out of 100' = <u>20 ÷ 100</u> = $\frac{20}{100}$

(That's how you work it out in the method shown above)

2) <u>'OF' means '×'</u>

In maths, the word 'of' can always be replaced with '×' for working out the answer.
(as shown in the above method)

Important Example — % Discount

E.g.   A radio is priced at £8.50 but there is a discount of 20% available.
FIND THE REDUCED PRICE OF THE RADIO.

<u>ANSWER:</u>

First find 20% of £8.50 using the method above:

1) 20% of £8.50

2) $\frac{20}{100} \times 8.5$

3) 20 ÷ 100 × 8.5 = 1.7 = <u>£1.70</u>

It's money, so 1.7 on the calculator display is £1.70.

This is the <u>DISCOUNT</u> so we <u>take it away</u> to get the final answer: £8.50 − £1.70 = <u>£6.80</u>

Reality TV show error #52 — it's impossible to give 110%......

Always use the <u>three-part method</u> for working out percentages. Have a go at this one:

1) A bank charges interest at 12% per year. If £1000 is borrowed for one year, how much interest will be charged?

Ratio

There are lots of Exam questions which at first sight seem completely different but in fact they can all be done using the GOLDEN RULE...

DIVIDE FOR ONE, THEN TIMES FOR ALL

| Example 1: | "5 pints of Milk cost £1.30. How much will 3 pints cost?" |

The GOLDEN RULE says:

DIVIDE FOR ONE, THEN TIMES FOR ALL

which means:

Divide the price by 5 to find how much FOR ONE PINT, then multiply by 3 to find how much FOR 3 PINTS.

So...
> £1.30 ÷ 5 = 0.26 = 26p (for 1 pint)
> ×3 = 78p (for 3 pints)

My favourite cereal is muesli.

| Example 2: | "Divide £400 in the ratio 5:3" |

The GOLDEN RULE says:

DIVIDE FOR ONE, THEN TIMES FOR ALL

The trick with this type of question is to add together the numbers in the RATIO to find how many PARTS there are: 5 + 3 = 8 parts.

Now use The Golden Rule:

Divide the £400 by 8 to find how much it is for ONE PART, then multiply by 5 and by 3 to find how much 5 PARTS ARE and how much 3 PARTS ARE.

So...
> £400 ÷ 8 = £50   (for 1 part)
> ×5 = £250   (for 5 parts)
> ×3 = £150   (for 3 parts)
>
> So £400 split in the ratio 5:3 is £250 : £150

The Three Mathsketeers say "divide for one, then times for all"...

Smug gits. It's a simple rule — the trick is knowing when to use it. Learning the examples above will help.
1) If seven pencils cost 98p, how much will 4 pencils cost?
2) Divide £2400 in the ratio 5:7.

Ratio

There's just so much great stuff to say about ratios. I couldn't possibly fit it onto only one page...

| Example 3: | "£9100 is to be split in the ratio 2:4:7. Find the 3 amounts." |

Remember — the key word here is PARTS — concentrate on 'parts' and it all becomes painless:

1) ADD UP THE PARTS:
   The ratio 2:4:7 means there will be a total of 13 parts
   i.e. 2+4+7 = 13 PARTS

2) FIND THE AMOUNT FOR ONE "PART"
   Just divide the total amount by the number of parts:
   £9100 ÷ 13 = £700 (= 1 PART)

3) HENCE FIND THE THREE AMOUNTS:
   2 parts = 2×700 = £1400,
   4 parts = 4×700 = £2800,
   7 parts = £4900

Reducing Ratios to their Simplest Form

You reduce ratios just like you'd reduce fractions to their simplest form.

For the ratio 15:18, both numbers have a factor of 3, so divide them by 3 — that gives 5:6. We can't reduce this any further. So the simplest form of 15:18 is 5 : 6.

Treat them just like Fractions — use your Calculator if you can

Now this is really sneaky. If you stick in a fraction using the a^b_c button, your calculator automatically cancels it down when you press $=$.

So for the ratio 8:12, just press 8 a^b_c 12 $=$, and you'll get the reduced fraction $\frac{2}{3}$. Now you just change it back to ratio form ie. 2 : 3. Ace.

Ratio Nelson — didn't he proportionally divide the French at Trafalgar...

Oh I do make myself chuckle. Learn the 3 steps for proportional division.
Now turn over and write down what you've learned. Then try these:
1) Cement and sand are mixed in the ratio 1:3 to make mortar.
   How much sand is needed to make a 2 kg mix of mortar?
2) Divide £8400 in the ratio 5:3:4

Best Buys

A favourite type of question they like to ask you in Exams is comparing the 'value for money' of 2 or 3 similar items. Always follow the GOLDEN RULE...

> ### Divide by the PRICE in pence
> ### (to get the amount per penny)

Example:

The local 'Supplies 'n' Vittals' stocks three sizes of Jamaican Gooseberry Jam. The question is: Which of these represents 'THE BEST VALUE FOR MONEY'?

500 g at £1.08   350 g at 80p   100 g at 42p

ANSWER: the GOLDEN RULE says:

DIVIDE BY THE PRICE IN PENCE TO GET THE AMOUNT PER PENNY

So we shall:

$$500 \text{ g} \div 108\text{p} = \underline{4.6 \text{ g PER PENNY}}$$

$$350 \text{ g} \div 80\text{p} = \underline{4.4 \text{ g PER PENNY}}$$

$$100 \text{ g} \div 42\text{p} = \underline{2.4 \text{ g PER PENNY}}$$

So you can now see straight away that THE 500 g JAR is the best value for money because you get MORE JAM PER PENNY. (As you should expect, it being the big jar).

With any question comparing 'value for money', DIVIDE BY THE PRICE (in pence) and it will always be the BIGGEST ANSWER is the BEST VALUE FOR MONEY.

The other golden rule — never dunk a biscuit for longer than 3 seconds...

Learn the Golden Rule for finding a best buy, then cover it up and answer this little beauty:

Froggatt's 'Slugtail Soup' comes in three different sizes:

The 150 g tin at 87p, the 250 g tin at £1.37 and the Farmhouse Size, 750 g at £3.95.

Work out which one is the best value for money. (And don't just guess!)

Unit 1 — Statistics and Probability

Probability

Believe me, probability's not as bad as you think it is, but YOU MUST LEARN THE BASIC FACTS.

All Probabilities are between 0 and 1

Probabilities can only have values from 0 to 1 (including those values). You should be able to put the probability of any event happening on this scale of 0 to 1.

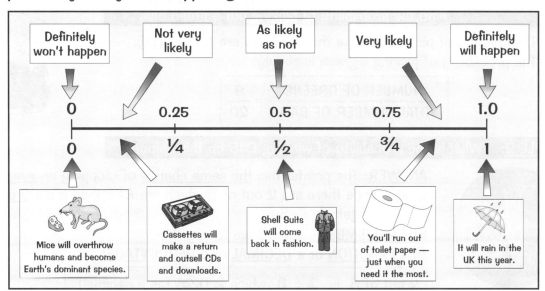

Remember you can give probabilities using FRACTIONS, DECIMALS or PERCENTAGES.

Equal Probabilities

When the different results all have the same chance of happening, then the probabilities will be EQUAL. These are the two cases which usually come up in Exams:

1) TOSSING A COIN:	Equal chance of getting a head or a tail (probability = $\frac{1}{2}$)
2) THROWING A DICE:	Equal chance of getting any of the numbers (probability = $\frac{1}{6}$)

I hope they don't ask me to toss this.

The Probability of the Opposite happening is just the rest of the probability that's left over

This is simple enough AS LONG AS YOU REMEMBER IT.
If the probability of something happening is, say, 0.3 then the chance of it NOT HAPPENING is 1 – 0.3 (= 0.7), i.e. it's what's left when you subtract it from 1.

Example: A loaded dice has a 0.25 chance of coming up TWO. What's the chance of it not coming up TWO?
Answer: 1 – 0.25 = 0.75. So, the chance of the dice not coming up TWO is 0.75.

The probability of death and taxes is 1...

Picking cards from a pack is another example of equal probabilities, and it might come up in your exam.
1) What is the probability of picking from a shuffled deck of cards (no jokers)
   a) An ace of any suit? b) A number less than 7? c) a red picture card? (remember, it's 52 cards in a pack).

Probability

There's more to probability than just tossing coins and rolling dice you know. Oh yes.

Unequal Probabilities

These make for more interesting questions. (Which means you'll get them in the Exam.)

EXAMPLE 1: "A bag contains 6 blue balls, 5 red balls and 9 green balls. Find the probability of picking out a green ball."

ANSWER: The chances of picking out the three colours are NOT EQUAL.
The probability of picking a green is simply:

$$\frac{\text{NUMBER OF GREENS}}{\text{TOTAL NUMBER OF BALLS}} = \frac{9}{20}$$

EXAMPLE 2: "What is the probability of winning £45 on this spinner?"

ANSWER: The pointer has the same chance of stopping on every sector...
... and since there are 2 out of 8 which are £45 then it's a 2 out of 8 chance of getting £45.

BUT REMEMBER ... you have to say this as a FRACTION or a DECIMAL or a PERCENTAGE:

2 out of 8 is 2 ÷ 8 which is 0.25 (as a decimal) or $\frac{1}{4}$ (as a fraction) or 25% (as a percentage)

Listing All Outcomes: 2 Coins, Dice, Spinners

A simple question you might get is to list all the possible results from tossing two coins or two spinners or a dice and a spinner, etc. Whatever it is, it'll be very similar to these, so LEARN THEM:

The possible outcomes from TOSSING TWO COINS are:
HH   HT   TH   TT

From TWO SPINNERS with 3 sides:

BLUE, 1	RED, 1	GREEN, 1
BLUE, 2	RED, 2	GREEN, 2
BLUE, 3	RED, 3	GREEN, 3

Try and list the possible outcomes METHODICALLY — to make sure you get them ALL.

You could list all the possible results in a sample space diagram — it's basically a posh name for a table. If you use one, you're less likely to miss out any outcomes.

This table uses columns for the colours and rows for the numbers. It doesn't matter which way round you do it though.

	Red	Blue	Green
1	1R	1B	1G
2	2R	2B	2G
3	3R	3B	3G

Spinning the number AND the colour spinner gives $3 \times 3 = 9$ different combinations altogether (since any number on the first spinner could come up with any colour on the second spinner). The sample space is a list of these 9 outcomes.

So the probability of spinning, say, a 2 and a GREEN (2G) is $\frac{1}{9}$.

Spinners fashion tip #56 — gold hot pants are an absolute must......

Spinners and bags of balls come up a lot in the exam. Don't panic if they use another example — you work it out in exactly the same way. Try this one: 1) What is the probability of picking a white puppy from a bag containing 3 black puppies, 4 brown puppies, 2 white puppies and one purple puppy?

Probability — Relative Frequency

This isn't the number of times your granny comes to visit. It's a way of working out <u>probabilities</u>. Since you asked, my granny visits twice a year. She says she'd like to visit more, but sleeping on the blow-up bed plays mischief with her bad back.

The Expected Frequency is What's Likely to Happen

Once you know the <u>probability</u> of something happening, you can predict <u>how many times</u> it will happen in a certain number of trials, e.g. the <u>number of sixes</u> you could expect if you rolled a fair dice <u>20 times</u>. This prediction is called the <u>EXPECTED FREQUENCY</u>.

EXPECTED FREQUENCY =	NUMBER OF TIMES you are going to do something (the number of trials)	×	The PROBABILITY of the outcome happening

$$= \quad 20 \quad \times \quad \frac{1}{6} \quad = 3.33...$$
$$\text{(basically 3 times)}$$

Relative Frequency — Do the Experiment Again and Again

Expected frequency only works if something is <u>unbiased</u>, e.g. if you're using a <u>fair dice</u> in the example above. To work out <u>relative frequency</u> you need to do an experiment <u>over and over again</u> and then do a quick calculation. (Remember, an experiment could just mean rolling a dice.)

The Formula for Relative Frequency

$$\text{Probability of something happening} \ = \ \frac{\text{Number of times it has happened}}{\text{Number of times you tried}}$$

You can work out the relative frequency as a <u>fraction</u> but usually <u>decimals</u> are best.

The important thing to remember is:

> The more times you do the experiment, the more accurate the probability will be.

Example:

Number of Times the dice was rolled	10	20	50	100
Number of threes rolled	2	5	11	23
Relative Frequency	$\frac{2}{10} = 0.2$	$\frac{5}{20} = 0.25$	$\frac{11}{50} = 0.22$	$\frac{23}{100} = 0.23$

So, what's the probability of rolling a 3? We've got <u>4 possible answers</u>, but the best is the one worked out using the <u>highest number of dice rolls</u>. This makes the probability of rolling a three on this dice <u>0.23</u>.

And since for a fair, unbiased dice, the probability of rolling a three is $\frac{1}{6}$ (about 0.17), then our dice is probably <u>biased</u>.

Dice rolls — a crunchy pack lunch alternative...

Learn the formulas on this page, then it's time to test yourself with a question. Oh, like the one here...

1) A 3-sided spinner is spun 100 times – it lands on red 43 times, blue 24 times and green the other times. Calculate the relative frequency of each outcome.

Data

Data is what statistics is all about. You've got to collect it, process it and then interpret it.

Choose an Appropriate Source of Data

1) The first thing to do when you're collecting data is to identify exactly what data you need.

2) Then you need to weigh up the pros and cons of using either primary or secondary data:

PRIMARY data is data you've collected.

1) There are the two main ways you can gather primary data:
A SURVEY, e.g. a questionnaire.
An EXPERIMENT — when you measure how one thing changes when you change something else.

2) Primary data is often RAW DATA — data that hasn't been processed.

SECONDARY data is collected by someone else.

1) There are lots of ways you can get hold of secondary data e.g. from newspapers, the internet, databases and historical records.

2) Secondary data has normally been PROCESSED before you get it e.g. it could be presented as a percentage, graph or table.

Data can be Quantitative or Qualitative

1) Quantitative data is anything that you can measure with a number.

2) For example, heights of people, the time taken to complete a task or the mass of things.

3) Quantitative data tends to be easier to analyse than qualitative data.

1) Qualitative data is data that uses words to describe it — it doesn't use any numbers.

2) For example, gender, eye colour or how nice a curry is.

3) This sort of data is usually harder to analyse than quantitative data.

Quantitative Data is Either Discrete or Continuous

DISCRETE DATA is data that can be measured exactly.

1) If your data is something that's countable in whole numbers or can only take certain individual values, it's called discrete data.

2) E.g. the number of points scored in a game, the number of people going into a shop on a Saturday and the number of pages in this book.

CONTINUOUS DATA is data that can take any value in an interval.

1) If your data is something that could always be more accurately measured, it's continuous data.

2) E.g. the height of this page. The height is 297 mm to the nearest mm, but you'd get a more accurate height if you measured to the nearest 0.1 mm or 0.01 mm or 0.001 mm or 0.0001 mm, etc...

3) Other examples are the weight of a pumpkin, the age of a chicken and the length of a carrot.

Sorry, I can't date 'er — she's just not my type...

Nowt too complicated here, just a few more definitions to learn. Once you've got 'em, try this question:

1) Say whether this data is qualitative, discrete or continuous:
   a) The number of spectators at a rugby match.
   b) The colours of pebbles on a beach.
   c) The nationalities of people visiting a park on a certain day.
   d) The lengths of fish in a pond.

Data

My top tip for revision: keep yourself awake with a big vat of <u>coffee</u>, a regular blare of <u>loud music</u> and an occasional dance of the <u>hokey cokey</u>. If you don't fancy that, carry on with this page...

You can Split your Data into Classes

1) If you're collecting <u>lots of data</u>, or your data's <u>spread out</u> over a large range, you can make it more manageable by <u>grouping it</u> into different <u>classes</u>.

2) When you do this, it's important that you <u>define the classes well</u> so <u>none of them overlap</u> — this means that each bit of data can <u>only</u> be put into <u>one class</u>.

Age in completed years	0 – 19	20 – 39	40 – 59	60 – 79	80 – 99
Number of people	6	13	14	8	9

3) The <u>problem</u> with grouping data is that you <u>lose</u> some of the <u>accuracy</u> of the data because you don't know what the <u>exact data values</u> are any more.

Sampling — Cheaper and Easier than Asking Everyone

1) For any statistical project, you need to find out information about a group of people or things. This group is called the **POPULATION**. Examples of populations are things like all the pupils in a school, or all the people who have access to the internet.

2) You collect information about a population by doing a **SURVEY** — you can collect data from the <u>whole population</u> or from a **SAMPLE** (<u>part of the population</u>).

3) Surveying a sample is a relatively <u>easy</u> way of finding out about a population. You can use the data you collect to make <u>estimates</u> and <u>draw conclusions</u> about the <u>whole population</u>.

4) There are <u>pros</u> and <u>cons</u> of using <u>sample data</u>:

PROS It's a lot <u>quicker</u>, <u>cheaper</u> and often <u>more practical</u> than doing a survey of the entire population.

CONS You <u>don't</u> have information about <u>every member</u> of the population.

It's really important that your sample is **REPRESENTATIVE** — it has to be <u>unbiased</u> and <u>big enough</u> (see p.14).

Survey Questions can Have a Fixed Number of Answers

Some <u>survey questions</u> have a <u>fixed number</u> of possible answers — these could be yes/no or tick box questions.

The good thing about closed questions is that you can <u>easily process</u> the data collected. Also, if the question is well designed, the responses <u>won't be ambiguous</u> at all. But, the answers are <u>limited</u> to the options given.

1) Are you under 18 years of age?
2) Tick the mode of transport you use to get to school.
Bus ☐ Car ☐ Bicycle ☐
Walking ☐ Other ☐

When getting a sample — size matters...

...so that it's more representative. Have a go at this question: explain whether a survey on the music listening preferences of a school using a Year 7 class as a sample is likely to be representative.

Data

Questionnaires are a good way of collecting data — they're <u>cheap</u> and <u>easy</u> to give to lots of people.

Design your Questionnaire Carefully

Bear these <u>six points</u> in mind when you <u>design</u> a questionnaire:

1 MAKE SURE YOUR QUESTIONS ARE RELEVANT

It's no good asking really <u>fascinating</u> questions if the answers aren't going to be useful.

2 QUESTIONS SHOULD BE <u>CLEAR</u>, <u>BRIEF</u> AND <u>EASY TO UNDERSTAND</u>

Your best bet is to assume that the people answering them are really stupid.

3 ALLOW FOR <u>ALL POSSIBLE ANSWERS</u> TO YOUR QUESTION

E.g. "What is your favourite subject: Maths, English or Science?" is difficult to answer <u>truthfully</u> if you like Art best — to help, you could add an "other" category.

4 QUESTIONS SHOULDN'T BE <u>LEADING</u> OR <u>BIASED</u>

<u>Leading</u> or <u>biased questions</u> are ones that <u>suggest</u> what answer is wanted.
For example: "You do agree that thrash metal is really good music?"
A better question would be "What type of music do you prefer to listen to?"

5 QUESTIONS SHOULD BE <u>UNAMBIGUOUS</u>

Here's an example: "Do you play computer games a lot?"
This question could be <u>interpreted differently</u> by different people. One person could answer <u>yes</u>, while another who plays the same amount could answer <u>no</u>. A <u>better question</u> is "How many hours do you play computer games per week?" because it isn't open to different interpretations.

6 PEOPLE MAY NOT ANSWER QUESTIONS <u>TRUTHFULLY</u>

This is often because they're <u>embarrassed</u> about the answer. For example "What is your age?" might be a <u>sensitive question</u> for some people. You can get round this by using groups so they don't have to answer with their exact age.

Make Sure your Data is Reliable and Not Biased

1) When you sample a population it's <u>important</u> to make sure the sample <u>fairly represents</u> the <u>whole population</u>. This means any <u>conclusions</u> you draw from the data can be <u>applied</u> to the <u>whole population</u>.

2) A <u>BIASED</u> study is one that <u>doesn't fairly represent</u> the <u>whole population</u>. To avoid bias you need to:

   - Use a <u>REPRESENTATIVE SAMPLE</u> — in other words, make sure that all the <u>different groups</u> of people are represented in your sample and that no group or type of person is <u>excluded</u>.
   - Select your sample at <u>RANDOM</u>. Something is chosen at random when <u>every item</u> in the group has an <u>equal chance</u> of being chosen.

3) A <u>bigger sample</u> is <u>better</u> because it's more likely to be <u>representative</u>, but <u>only</u> if you're sampling the <u>right population</u>. It'll provide <u>more reliable data</u> — but it might be <u>less practical</u> to <u>collect</u>.

Who wants to collect a questionnaire...

... is the (not so exciting) quiz spin-off. Make sure you learn this page and then try this question...

1) Give one criticism of each of these questions: a) Do you watch a lot of television?
   b) Do you agree that maths is the most important subject taught in schools?
   c) What is your favourite drink? Answer A, B or C.   A) Tea   B) Milk   C) Coffee

Mean, Median, Mode and Range

If you don't manage to learn the 4 basic definitions then you'll be passing up on some of the easiest marks in the whole Exam. It can't be that difficult can it?

1) MODE = MOST common

Mode = most (emphasise the 'o' in each when you say them)

2) MEDIAN = MIDDLE value

Median = mid (emphasise the m*d in each when you say them)

3) MEAN = TOTAL of items ÷ NUMBER of items

Mean is just the average, 'but it's mean 'cos you have to work it out'

4) RANGE = How far from the smallest to the biggest

THE GOLDEN RULE:

Mean, median, mode and range should be easy marks but even people who've gone to the incredible extent of learning them still manage to lose marks in the Exam because they don't do this one vital step:

Always REARRANGE the data in ASCENDING ORDER

(and then check you have the same number of entries)

Example:

"Find the mean, median, mode and range of these numbers:"

2, 5, 3, 2, 6, -4, 0, 9, -3, 1, 6, 3, -2, 3   (14)

1) FIRST... rearrange them: -4, -3, -2, 0, 1, 2, 2, 3, 3, 3, 5, 6, 6, 9   (✓14)

2) MEAN = $\frac{total}{number}$ = $\dfrac{-4-3-2+0+1+2+2+3+3+3+5+6+6+9}{14}$

= 31 ÷ 14 = 2.21

3) MEDIAN = the middle value (only when they're arranged in order of size, that is).

When there are two middle numbers, as in this case, then the median is halfway between the two middle numbers.

-4, -3, -2, 0, 1, 2, 2, 3, 3, 3, 5, 6, 6, 9
← seven numbers this side   seven numbers this side →
Median = 2.5

4) MODE = most common value, which is simply 3. (Or you can say "The modal value is 3")

5) RANGE = distance from lowest to highest value, i.e. from -4 up to 9, = 13

Don't forget the order — socks and then shoes...

Trust me — it's easily done. Learn the four definitions and the Golden Rule, then cover this page and write them all down from memory. Then be a clever bunny and use everything you've learnt to find the mean, median, mode and range for this set of data: 1, 3, 14, -5, 6, -12, 18, 7, 23, 10, -5, -14, 0, 25, 8

Frequency Tables

Frequency tables can either be done in rows or in columns of numbers. They can be quite confusing, but they're not too bad if you learn these key points:

1) The word FREQUENCY just means HOW MANY, so a frequency table is nothing more than a 'How many in each group' table.
2) The FIRST ROW (or column) just gives the GROUP LABELS.
3) The SECOND ROW (or column) gives the ACTUAL DATA.
4) To find the MEAN you have to WORK OUT A THIRD ROW (or column) and then **MEAN = 3rd Row total ÷ 2nd Row Total**

Example:

Here is a typical frequency table in ROW FORM and COLUMN FORM:

Row Form

No. of Sisters	0	1	2	3	4	5	6
Frequency	7	15	12	8	3	1	0

Column Form

No. of Sisters	Frequency
0	7
1	15
2	12
3	8
4	3
5	1
6	0
Totals	46

The mode and range are easy to find from the table:

The MODE is just the group with the most entries: i.e 1

The 2nd row tells us there are people with anything from 'no sisters' right up to 'five sisters' (but not 6 sisters). So the RANGE is 5 – 0 = 5

To find the mean for the data, you need to add an extra row:

No. of Sisters	0	1	2	3	4	5	6	Totals	
Frequency	7	15	12	8	3	1	0	46	(People asked)
No. × Frequency	0	15	24	24	12	5	0	80	(Sisters)

Now from the table:

$$\text{MEAN} = \frac{\text{3rd row total}}{\text{2nd row total}} = \frac{80}{46} = 1.74 \text{ (sisters per person)}$$

Mean sisters

My table has 5 columns, 6 rows and 4 legs...

Learn the rules for frequency tables, then turn over and write them down to see what you know. The best way of getting your head round this is to practise doing it, so have a go yourself. You could ask your class how many times they've been to Bury. Then put the results in a frequency table.

Averages and Grouped Data

Frequency tables often group data together to make it easier to understand. I, on the other hand, like to write with my eyes closed to make it harder to understand. But that's just me.

Example 1:

The marks of 28 students in a test (out of 80) were:

63, 45, 44, 52, 58,
49, 48, 22, 37, 34,
44, 49, 66, 73, 69,
32, 49, 29, 55, 57,
30, 72, 59, 46, 70,
39, 27, 40

As a Grouped Table

Marks	Tally	Frequency
$0 \leq x \leq 10$		
$11 \leq x \leq 20$		
$21 \leq x \leq 30$	IIII	4
$31 \leq x \leq 40$	̶H̶H̶	5
$41 \leq x \leq 50$	̶H̶H̶ III	8
$51 \leq x \leq 60$	̶H̶H̶	5
$61 \leq x \leq 70$	IIII	4
$71 \leq x \leq 80$	II	2
		28

Example 2:

The weights (in kg) of a bunch of 20 school kids are shown below.

67.3, 45.6, 47.7, 65.0, 54.2,
76.5, 44.6, 34.3, 69.8, 53.9,
32.3, 54.5, 78.9, 59.8, 57.4,
30.0, 79.1, 46.2, 66.0, 51.6

As a Grouped Table

Weight w (kg)	Tally	Frequency
$30 \leq w < 40$	III	3
$40 \leq w < 50$	̶H̶H̶	4
$50 \leq w < 60$	IIII I	6
$60 \leq w < 70$	IIII	4
$70 \leq w < 80$	III	3
		20

Reading the Intervals

In the top table, '$0 \leq x \leq 10$' means x is either between 0 and 10 or it is one of those values.

In the bottom table, '$30 \leq w < 40$' means w is between 30 and 40 or it could equal 30, but It can't equal 40 (40 would go in the next group).

Mid-Interval Values

The mid-interval value is exactly what you'd expect — the number exactly in the middle of the interval. You do need to be a little careful when working them out though.

1) For simple ones like $10 \leq x < 20$, it's pretty obvious — 15 is the mid-interval value.

2) For something like $11 \leq x \leq 20$, it's a bit more awkward.

Use this simple method: work out the difference, half it, then add this to the bottom number. Here, the difference is 9, half that is 4.5. So the mid-interval value is $11 + 4.5 = 15.5$

Tallya what, we'll have an interval now...

Learn how to draw frequency tables and make sure you know how to work out mid-interval values. They're easy to do, but also easy to get slightly wrong, so it's worth getting some practice.

Averages and Grouped Data

Now onto the slightly trickier stuff — so make sure you follow the steps below.

'Estimating' The Mean using Mid-Interval Values

You need to be able to estimate the mean for data in a grouped frequency table.
Note you can only estimate the mean because you don't know the actual values.

The method is a bit fiddly at first, but it's easy once you've learnt it:

1) Add a 3rd row and enter MID-INTERVAL VALUES for each group.
2) Add a 4th row and multiply FREQUENCY × MID-INTERVAL VALUE for each group.
3) Work out the TOTALS of rows 2 and 4.
4) Get the mean by dividing ROW 4 TOTAL by ROW 2 TOTAL.

See P.17 for how to find mid-interval values.

Note — if your table is arranged like the ones on the previous page, you'll need to add extra columns rather than rows...

Example:

The table below shows the distribution of weights of 60 children.
Find the modal class and estimate the mean.

Weight (kg)	$30 \leq w < 40$	$40 \leq w < 50$	$50 \leq w < 60$	$60 \leq w < 70$	$70 \leq w < 80$
Frequency	8	16	18	12	6

The modal class is just the one with the highest frequency: $50 \leq w < 60$ kg

To find the mean, add two rows to the table as described above:

Weight (kg)	$30 \leq w < 40$	$40 \leq w < 50$	$50 \leq w < 60$	$60 \leq w < 70$	$70 \leq w < 80$	Totals
Frequency	8	16	18	12	6	60
Mid-Interval Value	35	45	55	65	75	—
Frequency × Mid-Interval Value	280	720	990	780	450	3220

Now, just divide the totals to get an estimate of the mean:

$$\text{Mean} = \frac{\text{Overall Total (Final Row)}}{\text{Frequency Total (2nd Row)}} = \frac{3220}{60} = \underline{53.7}$$

The median can't be found exactly but you can say which class it's in.
If all the data were put in order, the 30th/31st entries would be in the $50 \leq w < 60$ kg class.

This page auditioned for Britain's next top modal...

It didn't get through — but I think I'll try again next year. Learn all the stuff on this page, then turn over and write down everything you've just learned. Good, clean fun. Then have a go at these...

1) Estimate the mean for this table: 2) State the modal class and the class containing the median.

Length L (cm)	$15.5 \leq L < 16.5$	$16.5 \leq L < 17.5$	$17.5 \leq L < 18.5$	$18.5 \leq L < 19.5$
Frequency	12	18	23	8

Tables, Charts and Graphs

Make sure you know how to <u>represent your data</u> in different types of <u>charts</u>, <u>tables</u> and <u>graphs</u>.

1) Line Graphs and Frequency Polygons

A <u>line graph</u> is just a set of points joined with straight lines.

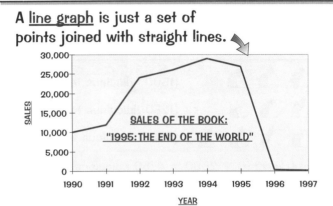

A <u>frequency polygon</u> looks similar and is used to show the information from a frequency table like the ones on p.16 and p.17.

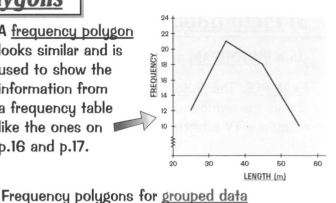

Frequency polygons for <u>grouped data</u> use the <u>mid-interval value</u> of <u>each class</u>.

EXAMPLE This frequency table shows the heights of 12 plants in a biology experiment. <u>Draw</u> a <u>frequency polygon</u> using this data.

Height	$0 \leq h < 5$	$5 \leq h < 10$	$10 \leq h < 15$	$15 \leq h < 20$
Frequency	3	5	2	2

1) You need to work out the <u>mid-interval values</u> for each class of heights first:

Height	$0 \leq h < 5$	$5 \leq h < 10$	$10 \leq h < 15$	$15 \leq h < 20$
Mid-interval value	2.5	7.5	12.5	17.5
Frequency	3	5	2	2

2) Then <u>PLOT</u> the mid-interval value of each class against its frequency and join the points with <u>straight lines</u> (because it's a <u>polygon</u> rather than a curve).

<u>Frequency</u> is <u>always</u> on the y-axis.

The <u>highest peak</u> tells you the group with the highest frequency — 5-10 cm class.

Values on the x-axis are the <u>class boundaries</u>.

2) Two-Way Tables

These are a bit like frequency tables but they show <u>two</u> different things:

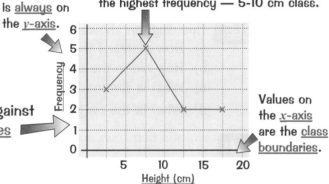

EXAMPLE: "Use this table to work out how many
(a) <u>right-handed people</u> and
(b) <u>left-handed women</u> there were in this survey."

	Women	Men	TOTAL
Left-handed		27	63
Right-handed	164	173	
TOTAL	200	200	400

ANSWER:

(a) Either: (i) <u>add up</u> the number of right-handed women and the number of right-handed men. So that's $164 + 173 =$ <u>337 right-handed people</u>.
Or: (ii) <u>take away</u> the total number of left-handed people from the total number of people. So that's $400 - 63 =$ <u>337 right-handed people</u>.

(b) Either: (i) take away the number of right-handed women from the total number of women. That's $200 - 164 =$ <u>36 left-handed women</u>.

Or: (ii) take away the left-handed men from the total number of left-handed people. Which would be $63 - 27 =$ <u>36 left-handed women</u>.

No animals were harmed in the making of the lion graph above...

Ho. Ho. Have a go at sketching examples of each type of table or graph — just make up some data. Then copy out the two-way table, close the book and fill in the blanks. Check the numbers add up.

Tables, Charts and Graphs

Ooo, now it's time for a graph where you get to draw <u>pretty pictures</u>. And some other types, but they're not as much fun. You've still got to know them though.

3) Pictograms — these use <u>pictures</u> instead of <u>numbers</u>.

In a <u>PICTOGRAM</u> each picture or symbol represents a certain number of items.

<u>EXAMPLE:</u> The <u>pictogram</u> opposite shows the number of talking cats used in ridiculous **TV** adverts in a 3-month period:

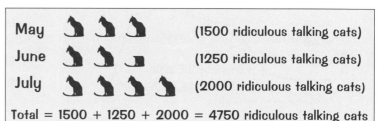

May	(1500 ridiculous talking cats)
June	(1250 ridiculous talking cats)
July	(2000 ridiculous talking cats)

= 500 talking cats

Total = 1500 + 1250 + 2000 = 4750 ridiculous talking cats

4) Stem and Leaf Diagrams

<u>Stem and leaf</u> diagrams are a bit like bar charts (see p.22), but more confusing. They're supposed to be easy to read, but they're not. So <u>LEARN</u> this example.

<u>EXAMPLE:</u> This diagram shows the ages of my school teachers.
a) How many of the teachers are in their forties?
b) How old is the oldest teacher?
c) What is the median age?
d) What is the range of ages?

```
3 | 3 5
4 | 0 5 7 8
5 | 1 4 9
6 | 1 3
```
Key: 5 | 4 means 54

The key tells you how to read the diagram. A 5 in the stem and a 4 in the leaf means 54.

<u>ANSWER:</u>

<u>Step 1:</u>
Write down all the ages of the teachers, using the key.

33, 35,
40, 45, 47, (48),
51, 54, 59,
61, (63)

<u>Step 2:</u>
Answer the question.

a) <u>four</u>
b) <u>63</u>
c) <u>48</u>
d) <u>30</u>

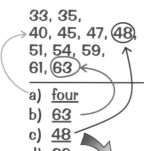

<u>Range</u> is simple — you can easily see the <u>smallest</u> and <u>largest ages</u> for each class.
So, the range is = 63 – 33 = <u>30 years</u>.

The <u>median</u> age of the teachers is either the middle value (or halfway between the two middle values) — it's easy to read these values off the diagram as the ages are already presented in <u>ascending order</u>.

If stem and leaf diagrams be the food of love, I wanna be single...

Ey up, that was a bit cultured wasn't it. Learn all about <u>pictograms</u> and <u>stem and leaf</u> diagrams, then...
1) Draw a stem and leaf diagram for this data: 3, 16, 14, 22, 7, 11, 26, 17, 12, 19, 20, 6, 13, 24, 26
2) Find the median and range of the data set.

Scatter Graphs

5) Scatter Graphs

A <u>SCATTER GRAPH</u> is used to show how two categories of data are related. If they're <u>closely related</u> then you get a <u>nice straight line</u>. If they're <u>not closely related</u>, you get a load of <u>messy-looking points</u>.

If the two categories are <u>closely related</u> (a straight-line) you say the data has <u>strong correlation</u>. If they <u>aren't related at all</u>, with the points all over the place, then you say there's <u>no correlation</u>. When you have strong correlation you can draw a <u>line of best fit</u> roughly through the <u>middle</u> of the points.

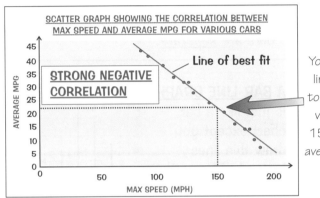

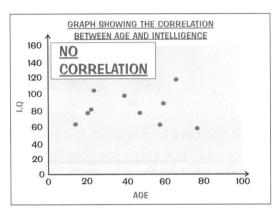

You can use the line of best fit to predict other values, e.g. at 150 MPH you'd average 22 MPG.

1) If the points form a line sloping <u>UPHILL</u> from left to right, then there is <u>POSITIVE CORRELATION</u>, which means that both things increase or decrease together.

2) If the points form a line sloping <u>DOWNHILL</u> from left to right, then there is <u>NEGATIVE CORRELATION</u>, which just means that as one thing increases the other decreases.

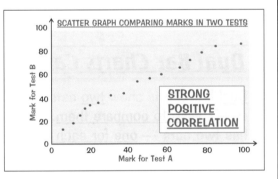

A Correlation doesn't always mean that one thing Causes another

If a change in one variable <u>CAUSES</u> a change in the other variable, they're said to have a <u>CAUSAL LINK</u>, e.g. a rise in the temperature outside could cause an increase in ice cream sales.

You have to be <u>VERY CAREFUL</u> though. Just because there's a correlation between two things, it <u>doesn't</u> necessarily mean there's a causal link — there could be a <u>third factor</u> involved.

For example, the number of pairs of sunglasses sold per week in a particular town is positively correlated with the amount of algae in a local pond. Neither one <u>causes</u> the other, though. Both of these increases are probably due to an increase in the amount of sunshine.

What soap do maths teachers watch — Correlation Street...

Recent studies have shown that there is strong positive correlation between time spent practising your evil laugh / cat stroking / beard combing and how successful you are as an evil genius. Learn the types of scatter graph on these two pages and have a go at drawing an example of each.

Bar Charts and Comparing Data

6) Bar Charts

Just watch out for when the bars should touch or not touch:

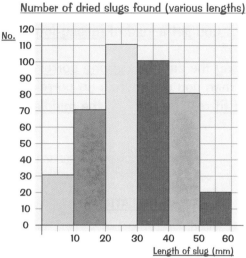

Number of dried slugs found (various lengths)

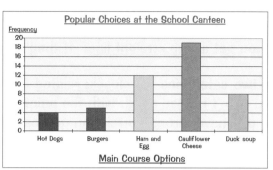

Popular Choices at the School Canteen

This bar chart compares <u>totally separate items</u> so the bars are <u>separate</u>.

ALL the bars in this chart are for LENGTHS and you must <u>put every possible length into one bar or the next</u> so there mustn't be any spaces.

You might get asked about <u>histograms</u> with <u>equal class intervals</u> in the exam — they're just the same as bar charts showing <u>continuous</u> data.

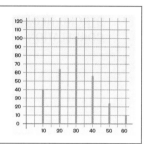

A <u>BAR-LINE GRAPH</u> is just like a bar chart except you draw thin lines instead of bars.

Dual Bar Charts Can be Used to Compare Data Sets

<u>Dual</u> bar charts show <u>two</u> sets of data at once so it's <u>easy to compare them</u>. Each category has two bars — <u>one for each data set</u>.

The dual bar chart on the right shows the favourite colours of a group of pupils, but it's split into two sets — <u>boys</u> and <u>girls</u>.

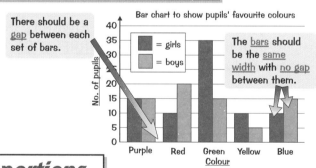

Bar chart to show pupils' favourite colours

There should be a <u>gap</u> between each set of bars.

The <u>bars</u> should be the <u>same width</u> with <u>no gap</u> between them.

Composite Bar Charts show Proportions

1) A <u>composite bar chart</u> has <u>single</u> bars, split into <u>sections</u>. The sections show <u>frequencies</u> for the different <u>categories</u> that make up the whole bar.

2) It's easy to read off <u>total frequencies</u> (the <u>heights</u> of the bars), as well as to <u>compare</u> different <u>categories</u>.

The composite bar chart on the right shows the number of men, women and children visiting a county show.

The data might be in <u>percentages</u>, with the height of the whole bar representing 100%.

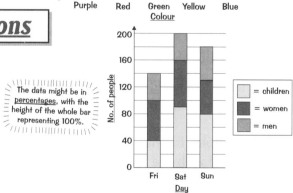

A sheep's favourite graph — the baaaa chart...

Woah, have another gander over this page, then test yourself with this delightful question.

1) Use the results from the "boring team names" quiz to draw a dual bar chart showing how the teams scored in each round.

Team	Green	Blue	Red	Yellow
Points — 1st round	24	15	20	25
Points — 2nd round	16	15	22	20

Pie Charts

In a similar way that you can make the correct combination of meat and pastry into a delicious pie, examiners can make Pie Charts into tricky exam questions. So learn the Golden Rule for Pie Charts:

The TOTAL of Everything = 360°

Remember that 360° is the trick for dealing with most Pie Charts

1) Relating Angles to Fractions

— you should just know these ones straight off:

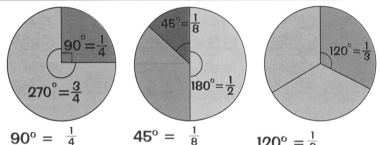

$$90° = \tfrac{1}{4}$$
$$270° = \tfrac{3}{4}$$

$$45° = \tfrac{1}{8}$$
$$180° = \tfrac{1}{2}$$

$$120° = \tfrac{1}{3}$$

For any angle the formula is:

$$\text{Fraction} = \frac{\text{Angle}}{360°}$$

And then cancel it down with your calculator (see the Calculation Tips pages)

If you have to measure an angle, you should expect it to be a nice round number like 90° or 180° or 120°, so don't go writing 89° or 181° or anything silly like that.

2) Relating Angles to Numbers of Other Things

Creature	Stick insects	Hamsters	Guinea pigs	Rabbits	Ducks	Total
Number	12	20	17	15	26	90
Angle		80°				360°

1) Add up all the numbers in each sector to get the TOTAL (=90).
2) Then find the MULTIPLIER (or divider) that you need to turn your total into 360°. For 90 → 360 as above, the MULTIPLIER is 4.
3) Now MULTIPLY EVERY NUMBER BY 4 to get the angle for each sector. E.g. the angle for hamsters will be 20 × 4 = 80°.

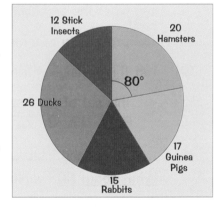

3) Use the Total to Find the Other Numbers

1) In the pie chart on the right, the total number of pets = 9
2) So you simply divide 360° by 9 = 40° — this represents one pet.
3) Then you divide each of the given angles by 40° to get the number of pets for that angle.
4) The final bit of pie is what's left over: 9 – 2 – 3 = 4 pet dogs.

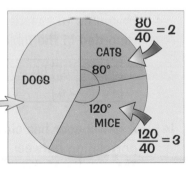

I bet you were expecting a joke about pies here...

... I'm far too witty to lower myself to making jokes about pies on a page about pie charts — that's much too obvious. There's just no need to go on and on about tasty steak-filled pies with scrumptious rich gravy on a bed of creamy mashed potato and a side order of mushy peas... mmm.

Anyway, while I'm off eating pies, you can display this data in a pie chart:

Football Team	Wigan A.	Luton	Man Utd	Others
No. of fans	53	15	30	22

Revision Summary for Unit 1 — Part 1

<u>WHAT YOU'RE SUPPOSED TO DO HERE</u> is put all the methods you
learnt in the first half of Unit 1 into practice to answer these questions.

1) Use the 🔲 button to <u>reduce</u> $^{12}/_{15}$ to its simplest form.

2) Convert 0.645 into a <u>fraction</u>.

3) Find the reduced price of a coat costing <u>£65</u> with a <u>15% discount</u>.

4) Sarah is ordering new stock for her clothes shop. The shop usually sells <u>red and blue scarves</u> in the ratio <u>5:8</u>. Sarah orders <u>150 red scarves</u>. How many <u>blue scarves</u> should she order?

5) Last week Rick ordered <u>5 pints of milk</u> from the milkman. His bill was <u>£2.35</u>. This week he orders <u>3 pints</u> of milk. How much will this week's bill be?

6) Charley loves ham. Two different sized tins of Froggatt's ham are on sale in his local shop. Which one is the 'Best Buy' for Charley?

7) Colin is designing a game for the school summer fair. He wants the players to have a <u>50% chance of winning</u>. He has a bag containing <u>3 red balls</u>, <u>5 green balls</u> and <u>7 black balls</u>. If you pick out a red or green ball you win a prize.
   a) What is the % chance of winning Colin's game?
   b) How can he change the game so that there's a 50% chance of winning?

8) If I toss a coin and throw a dice, <u>list all the possible outcomes</u> and say what the probability is of me getting <u>a HEAD and a SIX</u>.

9) The probability of a biased dice <u>giving a SIX</u> is <u>0.2</u>. What is the chance of it <u>NOT</u> giving a six?

10) List <u>three</u> things you need to bear in mind when designing a question for a questionnaire.

11) For this set of numbers: a) Find the <u>MODE</u>   b) Find the <u>MEDIAN</u>
    2, 6, 7, 12, 3, 7, 4, 15   c) Find the <u>MEAN</u>   d) Find the <u>RANGE</u>

12) In a frequency table what does $50 \leq w < 60$ mean? <u>Would you put 50 in this group</u>? <u>What about 60</u>, would it go in this group or the <u>next one up</u>, $60 \leq w < 70$?

13) Calum is writing an article on the <u>Skelly Crag half-marathon</u> for the local paper. He wants to include the average time taken. Use the times of all <u>1000</u> runners, recorded in the table below, to work out the <u>mean time taken</u>.

Time (min)	$60 < t \leq 90$	$90 < t \leq 120$	$120 < t \leq 150$	$150 < t \leq 180$	$180 < t \leq 210$	$210 < t \leq 240$
Frequency	15	60	351	285	206	83

14) A newspaper has claimed that a study shows a <u>strong positive correlation</u> between eating cheese and having nightmares. The results of the study are shown on the right.
    a) What does strong positive correlation mean?
    b) Do you agree with the newspaper claim?

15) Fiona has carried out a traffic survey as part of her Geography course work. She wants to present the information in a pie chart.
    a) <u>Complete Fiona's table</u>.
    b) Draw the <u>PIE CHART</u>.

Colour	Blue	Red	Yellow	White	Totals:
Number of Cars	12	15	4	9	40
Angle on Pie Chart					360°

Negative Numbers and Letters

Algebra — the very word is enough to strike fear into the heart of even the strongest person. But fear ye not, for here I shall show you how to create a shield of light powerful enough to deflect even the strongest rays of algebra, at a distance of over 30 metres. I call it the mirror...

Rule 1

+	+	makes	+
+	−	makes	−
−	+	makes	−
−	−	makes	+

Only to be used when:

1) Multiplying or dividing

e.g. $-2 \times 3 = -6$, $-8 \div -2 = +4$ $-4p \times -2 = +8p$

2) Two signs appear next to each other

e.g. $5 - -4 = 5 + 4 = 9$ $4 + -6 - -7 = 4 - 6 + 7 = 5$

Rule 2

Use the NUMBER LINE for ADDING OR SUBTRACTING:

E.g. "Simplify $4X - 8X - 3X + 6X$"

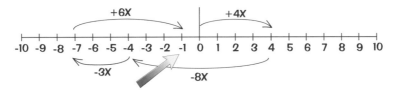

Good evening caller, you're through to the Number Line. What's your problem?

So $4X - 8X - 3X + 6X = \underline{-1X}$

Letters Multiplied Together

This is the super-slick notation they like to use in algebra which just ends up making life difficult for folks like you.   You've got to remember these five rules:

1) 'abc' means 'a×b×c'   The ×'s are often left out to make it clearer.

2) 'gn²' means 'g×n×n'   Note that only the n is squared, not the g as well.

3) '(gn)²' means 'g×g×n×n'   The brackets mean that **BOTH** letters are squared.

4) 'p(q − r)³' means 'p×(q − r) × (q − r) × (q − r)'   Only the brackets get cubed.

5) '−3²' is too ambiguous.   It should either be written $(-3)^2 = 9$, or $-(3^2) = -9$.

An **EXPRESSION** is just a bunch of letters and/or numbers added, subtracted, multiplied or divided together, for example y^2, $2 + 6$, $mx + 2$, $3y^3 - 2n$

Ahhh algebra, it's as easy as abc, or ab², or something like that...

Everyone knows Rule 1, but sometimes Rule 2 applies instead, so make sure you know both rules and when to use them. You also need to learn the 5 special cases of Letters Multiplied Together.

1) For each of a) to d), decide where Rule 1 and Rule 2 apply, and then work them out.

   a) -4×-3 b) $-4 + -5 + 3$ c) $(3X + -2X - 4X) \div (2 + -5)$ d) $120 \div -40$

2) If m=2 and n=-3, work out: a) mn^2 b) $(mn)^3$ c) $m(4+n)^2$ d) n^3 e) $3m^2n^3 + 2mn$

X and Y Coordinates

Graph questions can actually be quite fun. OK, maybe not fun exactly, but better than hopping blindfolded through a hail storm in just your pants. First, you need to get a grip of the basics...

The Four Quadrants

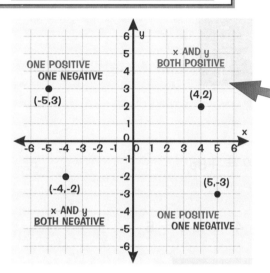

A graph has <u>four different regions</u> where the x- and y- coordinates are either <u>positive</u> or <u>negative</u>.

This is the easiest region by far because here <u>ALL THE COORDINATES ARE POSITIVE</u>.

You have to be <u>dead careful</u> in the <u>OTHER REGIONS</u> though, because the x- and y- coordinates could be <u>negative</u>, and that always makes life much more difficult.

X, Y Coordinates — Getting them in the Right Order

You must always give <u>COORDINATES</u> in brackets like this: (x, y)
And you always have to be real careful to get them <u>the right way round</u>, x first, then y.

Here are <u>THREE POINTS</u> to help you remember:

(x , y)

1) The two coordinates are always in <u>ALPHABETICAL ORDER, x then y</u>.

2) x is always the flat axis going <u>ACROSS</u> the page.
   In other words <u>'x is a..cross'</u>   Get it — x is a '×'. (Hilarious isn't it)

3) Remember it's always <u>IN THE HOUSE</u> (→) and then <u>UP THE STAIRS</u> (↑)
   so it's <u>ALONG first</u> and <u>then UP</u>, i.e. x-coordinate first, and then y-coordinate.

But what if you live in a bungalow?...

In that case, you just have to imagine where the stairs would be.
So, make sure you learn the <u>3 Rules for getting x and y</u>
<u>the right way round</u>. Then turn over and <u>write it all down</u>.

Write down the coordinates of the letters A to H on this graph:

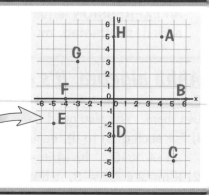

Straight-Line Graphs

If you thought I-spy was a fun, wait 'til you play 'recognise the straight-line graph from its equation'.

Horizontal and Vertical lines: "x = a" and "y = b"

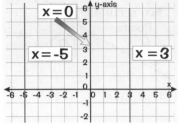

$x = a$ is a <u>vertical line</u> <u>through 'a'</u> on the x-axis

$y = a$ is a <u>horizontal line</u> <u>through 'a'</u> on the y-axis

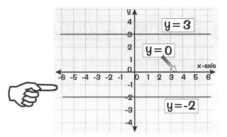

Don't forget: <u>the y-axis is also the line x=0</u>

Don't forget: <u>the x-axis is also the line y=0</u>

The Main Diagonals: "y = x" and "y = –x"

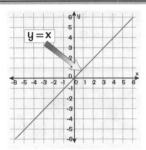

'$y = x$' is the <u>main diagonal</u> that goes <u>UPHILL</u> from left to right.

'$y = -x$' is the <u>main diagonal</u> that goes <u>DOWNHILL</u> from left to right.

Other Sloping Lines Through the origin: "y = ax" and "y = –ax"

<u>$y = ax$</u> and <u>$y = -ax$</u> are the equations for <u>A SLOPING LINE THROUGH THE ORIGIN</u>.

The value of '<u>a</u>' (known as the <u>gradient</u>) tells you the steepness of the line. The bigger 'a' is, the steeper the slope. A <u>MINUS SIGN</u> tells you it slopes <u>DOWNHILL</u>.

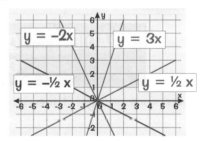

All Other Straight Lines

Other straight-line equations are a little more complicated. The next page shows you how to draw them, but the first step is identifying them in the first place.

Remember: All straight-line equations just contain '<u>something x, something y, and a number</u>'.

<u>Straight lines:</u>		<u>NOT straight lines:</u>	
$x - y = 0$	$y = 2 + 3x$	$y = x^3 + 3$	$2y - 1/x = 7$
$2y - 4x = 7$	$4x - 3 = 5y$	$1/y + 1/x = 2$	$x(3 - 2y) = 3$
$3y + 3x = 12$	$6y - x - 7 = 0$	$x^2 = 4 - y$	$xy + 3 = 0$

My favourite line's y = 3x, it gets the chicks every time...

OK, maybe not every time, but it's still worth learning all this stuff. When you think you know it, turn over the page and write down everything you've learned.

Straight-Line Graphs — Gradients

Time to hit the slopes. Well, find them anyway...

Finding the Gradient

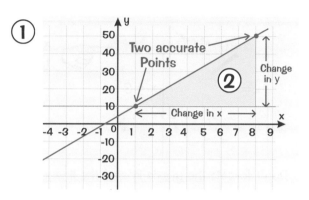

1) Find TWO ACCURATE POINTS

Both points should be in the <u>upper right quadrant</u> if possible (to keep all the numbers positive).

2) COMPLETE THE TRIANGLE as shown

3) Find the CHANGE IN Y and the CHANGE IN X

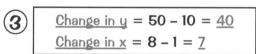

Make sure you subtract the x coords.
the <u>same way round</u> as you do the y coords.
E.g. y coord. of pt A − y coord. of pt B
<u>and</u> x coord of pt A − x coord of pt B
Make sure you do this using the SCALES on
the y- and x- axes, <u>not by counting cm</u>.
(So in the example shown, the change in y is
40 units from the y-axis.)

4) LEARN this formula, and use it:

$$\text{GRADIENT} = \frac{\text{CHANGE IN Y}}{\text{CHANGE IN X}} = \frac{\text{VERTICAL}}{\text{HORIZONTAL}}$$

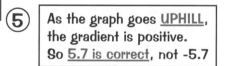

Make sure you get it the right way up too! Remember it's <u>VER</u>y <u>HO</u>t — <u>VER</u>tical over <u>HO</u>rizontal

5) Finally, is the gradient POSITIVE or NEGATIVE?

If it slopes <u>UPHILL</u> left → right (⟋) <u>then it's positive</u>
If it slopes <u>DOWNHILL</u> left → right (⟍) <u>then it's negative</u>
(so put a minus(−) in front of it)

⑤ As the graph goes <u>UPHILL</u>, the gradient is positive. So <u>5.7 is correct</u>, not -5.7

If you subtracted the coordinates the right way round, the sign should be correct. If it's not, go back and check what you've done.

Ch ch ch ch chaaaaaaaaaaaaaaaaaaaaaaaaaaaaaaanges...

<u>LEARN</u> the <u>FIVE STEPS</u> for finding a gradient then <u>turn over</u> and <u>WRITE THEM DOWN</u> from memory.
Plot these 3 points on a graph: (0,3) (2,0) (5,-4.5) and then join them up with a
straight line. Now carefully apply the <u>FIVE STEPS</u> to find the gradient of the line.

Real-life Graphs

Yay, just what you wanted to see — some more graphs...

Conversion Graphs

These are really easy. In the Exam you're likely to get a Conversion Graph
question which converts between things like £ → Dollars or mph → km/h, etc.

This graph converts between miles and kilometres

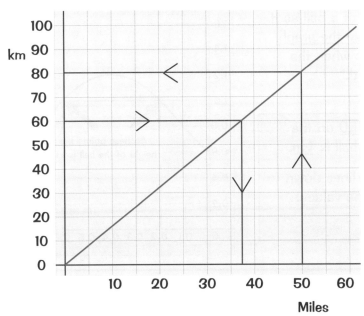

2 very typical questions:

1) How many miles is 60 km?

ANS: Draw a line <u>straight across</u> from
'60' on the 'km' axis 'til it <u>hits the line</u>,
then go <u>straight down</u> to the 'miles' axis
and read off the answer: <u>37.5 miles</u>

2) How many km is 50 miles?

ANS: Draw a line <u>straight up</u> from '50' on
the 'miles' axis 'til it <u>hits the line</u>,
then go <u>straight across</u> to the 'km' axis
and read off the answer: <u>80 km</u>

METHOD:

1) <u>Draw a line</u> from the <u>value</u> on one axis.
2) Keep going 'til you <u>hit the LINE</u>.
3) Then <u>change direction</u> and go straight to <u>the other axis</u>.
4) <u>Read off the new value</u> from the axis. <u>That's the answer</u>.

If you remember those 4 simple steps you really can't go wrong —
let's face it, Conversion Graphs are a doddle.

<u>Ready reckoner</u> graphs are basically any sort of chart that makes it <u>easy</u> to do <u>calculations</u>.
If you get asked to use one in the exam, don't panic — they're just like <u>conversion graphs</u>.

Convert revision hours into top grades...

These conversion graphs aren't too bad really.
But like anything maths-related — the more you practise,
the easier they'll become. So... learn this page, recite the
<u>METHOD</u> for using conversion graphs and then have a go
at this question:

1) Approximately how many pints is 3 litres?

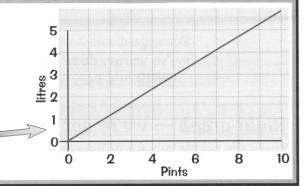

Real-life Graphs

It doesn't matter what type of graph you get asked questions about, distance vs time, chicken vs aliens — to read values from a graph you just need to follow the same easy method every time.

Getting Answers from your Graph

FOR A SINGLE CURVE OR LINE, you ALWAYS get the answer by drawing a straight line to the graph from one axis, and then down or across to the other axis, as shown here:

Example: "The graph shows the height of a ball as it is thrown through the air. Use the graph to find the approximate times when the ball was 1 m above the ground."

Method:

Draw a straight line across the graph at 1.0 on the y axis — this is where the height of the ball is 1 m.

The curve touches this line twice. Draw lines down to the x axis at these points and read off the values:

Time = 0.2 s and 0.6 s.

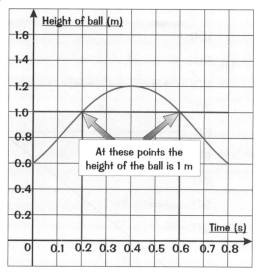

At these points the height of the ball is 1 m

What the Gradient of a Graph Means

No matter what the graph, THE MEANING OF THE GRADIENT is always simply:

(y-axis UNITS) PER (x-axis UNITS)

EXAMPLES:

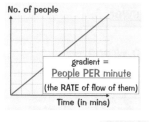

gradient = People PER minute (the RATE of flow of them)

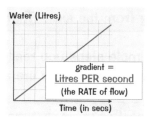

gradient = Litres PER second (the RATE of flow)

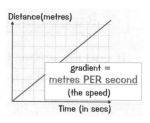

gradient = metres PER second (the speed)

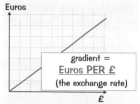

gradient = Euros PER £ (the exchange rate)

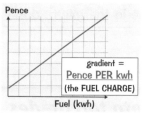

gradient = Pence PER kwh (the FUEL CHARGE)

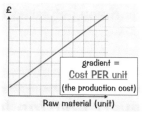

gradient = Cost PER unit (the production cost)

Some gradients have special names like Exchange Rate or Speed, but once you've written down 'something PER something' using the y-axis and x-axis UNITS, it's then pretty easy to work out what the gradient represents.

Right graph — we're not leaving here 'til I get some answers...

Learn the simple rule for getting answers from your graph and the meaning of the gradient of a graph. Then turn over... bla bla bla ... you know what to do...

Rounding Off

When you have <u>decimal numbers</u> you might have to round them off to the nearest <u>whole number</u>. The trouble is, they could also ask you to round them off to either <u>one decimal place</u> (or possibly <u>two decimal places</u>). This isn't too bad but you do have to learn some rules for it:

Basic Method

1) <u>Identify</u> the position of the LAST DIGIT.

2) Then look at the <u>next digit to the right</u> — called the DECIDER.

3) If the DECIDER is <u>5 or more</u>, then <u>ROUND-UP</u> the LAST DIGIT. If the DECIDER is <u>4 or less</u>, then leave the LAST DIGIT as it is.

<u>EXAMPLE</u>: What is 7.35 to 1 Decimal Place?

$$7.3\boxed{5} \quad = \quad \underline{7.4}$$

<u>LAST DIGIT</u> to be written (because we're rounding to 1 Decimal Place)

DECIDER

The <u>LAST DIGIT ROUNDS UP</u> to 4 because the <u>DECIDER</u> is <u>5 or more</u>

Decimal Places (D.P.)

1) To round off to <u>ONE DECIMAL PLACE</u>, the LAST DIGIT will be the one <u>just after the decimal point</u>.
2) There must be <u>NO MORE DIGITS</u> after the LAST DIGIT (not even zeros).

<u>EXAMPLES</u>

Round off 2.34 to 1 decimal place.	ANSWER:	<u>2.3</u>
Round off 4.57 to 1 decimal place.	ANSWER:	<u>4.6</u>
Round off 2.08 to 1 decimal place.	ANSWER:	<u>2.1</u>
Round off 2.346 to 2 decimal places.	ANSWER:	<u>2.35</u>

Rounding off decimal places — I totally dig it...

Personally, I quite like the rounding off methods on this page. They make it easier to explain to my numbers why I've rounded them up or down — I just <u>blame the rules</u>. They take it less personally then.

1) Round these numbers off to <u>1 decimal place</u>:
   a) 3.24   b) 1.78   c) 2.31   d) 0.46   e) 9.76

Unit 1 — Statistics and Probability

Rounding Off

If you thought that it was only numbers with decimal places that could be rounded off — then you're <u>wrong</u>. So very, very wrong. <u>Whole numbers</u> can be rounded off too. Yay.

Rounding Whole Numbers

The easiest ways to round off a number are:

1) 'To the nearest WHOLE NUMBER'   3) 'To the nearest HUNDRED'
2) 'To the nearest TEN'   4) 'To the nearest THOUSAND'

This isn't difficult so long as you remember the <u>2 RULES</u>:

> 1) The number <u>always lies between 2 POSSIBLE ANSWERS</u>,
>   Just <u>choose the one it's NEAREST TO</u>.
> 2) If the number is <u>exactly in the MIDDLE</u>, then <u>ROUND IT UP</u>.

<u>EXAMPLES</u>:

1) Give 231 to the nearest <u>TEN</u>.

ANSWER: 231 is between 230 and 240, but it is nearer to <u>230</u>

2) Give 145 to the nearest <u>HUNDRED</u>.

ANSWER: 145 is between 100 and 200, but it is nearer to <u>100</u>

3) Round 45.7 to the nearest <u>WHOLE NUMBER</u>.

ANSWER: 45.7 is between 45 and 46, but it is nearer to <u>46</u>

4) Round 4500 to the nearest <u>THOUSAND</u>.

ANSWER: 4500 is between 4000 and 5000. In fact it is exactly halfway between them. <u>So we ROUND IT UP</u> (see Rule 2 above) to <u>5000</u>

Significant Figures

> 1) The <u>MORE SIGNIFICANT FIGURES</u> a number has, the <u>MORE ACCURATE</u> it is.
> 2) The <u>NUMBER OF SIGNIFICANT FIGURES</u> is just <u>HOW MANY DIGITS</u>
>   the number has at the front <u>THAT ARE NOT ZERO</u>.

<u>EXAMPLES</u>:

234 has 3 significant figures   230 has 2 sig fig   900 has 1 sig fig
9810 has 3 sig fig   4000 has 1 sig fig   2.8 has 2 sig fig

Exam cheat wish #23 — all marks are rounded up to the nearest 100%...

Learn the <u>2 Rules for Rounding Whole Numbers</u> and the <u>2 Extra Rules about Significant Figures</u>. Simples.

1) Round these off to the <u>nearest whole number</u>:
   a) 3.4   b) 5.2   c) 1.84   d) 6.9   e) 3.26
2) Round these numbers to the stated number of significant figures:
   a) 352 to 2 s.f.   b) 465 to 1 s.f.   c) 12.38 to 3 s.f.   d) 0.03567 to 2 s.f.
3) Round these numbers off to the nearest hundred: a) 2865   b) 450   c) 123

Accuracy and Estimating

If you struggle with knowing what's appropriate, then this is the page for you. Read on to find out how to give <u>measurements</u> to an <u>appropriate degree of accuracy</u>. (If you're looking for tips on table manners try the GCSE Dining Etiquette book.)

Appropriate Accuracy

In the Exam you may well get a question asking for <u>'an appropriate degree of accuracy'</u> for a certain measurement. So how do you decide what is appropriate accuracy? The key to this is <u>the number of significant figures</u> (see P.32) that you give it to:

> 1) For fairly <u>casual measurements</u>, <u>2 SIGNIFICANT FIGURES</u> is most appropriate.

  E.g. <u>COOKING</u> — 250 g (2 sig. fig.) of sugar, <u>not</u> 253 g (3 S.F.), or 300 g (1 S.F.)
  <u>LENGTH OF A JOURNEY</u> — 450 miles or 25 miles or 3500 miles (All 2 S.F.)

> 2) For <u>MORE IMPORTANT OR TECHNICAL THINGS</u>, <u>3 SIGNIFICANT FIGURES</u> is essential.

  E.g. A <u>TECHNICAL FIGURE</u> — <u>34.2</u> miles per gallon, (<u>rather than</u> 34 mpg)

Estimating Calculations

As long as you realise what's expected, this is <u>VERY EASY</u>. People get confused because they <u>over-complicate it</u>. To <u>estimate</u> something this is all you do:

> 1) ROUND EVERYTHING OFF to nice easy CONVENIENT NUMBERS.
> 2) Then WORK OUT THE ANSWER using those nice easy numbers
> — and that's it!

You don't worry about the answer being 'wrong', because we're only trying to get a rough idea of the size of the proper answer, e.g. is it about 20 or about 200?

Don't forget though, in the Exam you'll need to <u>show all the steps you've done</u>, to prove you didn't just use a calculator.

Example 1: <u>ESTIMATE</u> the value of $\dfrac{127 + 49}{56.5}$ showing all your working.

> <u>ANSWER:</u>
>
> $\dfrac{127 + 49}{56.5} \approx \dfrac{130 + 50}{60} = \dfrac{180}{60} = 3$ ("$\approx$" means "<u>roughly equal to</u>")

Example 2: <u>ESTIMATE</u> the height of the giraffe showing all your working.

> <u>ANSWER:</u> Height of a man $\approx$ 2 m
> The giraffe is about two and a half times as tall as the man.
> So $2 \times 2.5 \approx 5$ m

Conversion Factors and Metric Units

Conversion Factors are a really good way of dealing with all sorts of questions — they're especially useful for converting between units. Luckily, the method is dead easy too.

Metric Units

1) <u>Length</u>   mm, cm, m, km
2) <u>Weight</u>   g, kg, tonnes

> **MEMORISE THESE KEY FACTS:**
>
> 1 cm = 10 mm   1 km = 1000 m   1 tonne = 1000 kg
>
> 1 m = 100 cm   1 kg = 1000 g

Method

1) Find the <u>CONVERSION FACTOR</u> (always easy).
2) <u>Multiply AND divide by it</u>.
3) Choose the <u>COMMON SENSE ANSWER</u>.

Hmm, seems plausible. But I tell you what'd really convince me — an example using slugs...

Example 1:

"A Giant Sea-slug called Kevin was washed up near Grange-Over-Sands. He was 18.6 m in length. How long is this in cm?"

> **Step 1)**   <u>Find the CONVERSION FACTOR</u>
> In this question the Conversion Factor = <u>100</u>
>   — simply because 1 m = <u>100</u> cm
>
> **Step 2)**   <u>MULTIPLY AND DIVIDE by the conversion factor:</u>
> 18.6 m × 100 = 1860 cm (makes sense)
> 18.6 m ÷ 100 = 0.186 cm (ridiculous)
>
> **Step 3)**   <u>Choose the COMMON SENSE answer:</u>
> Obviously the answer is that 18.6 m = <u>1860 cm</u>

Example 2:

"Hilda measures her desk at school. It's 562 mm wide. What is this in m?"

> **Step 1)**   <u>Find the CONVERSION FACTOR</u>
> In this question the Conversion Factor = <u>1000</u>
>   — because 1 m = <u>100</u> cm and 1 cm = <u>10</u> mm
>
> **Step 2)**   <u>MULTIPLY AND DIVIDE by the conversion factor:</u>
> 562 mm × 1000 = 562 000 m (silly)
> 562 mm ÷ 1000 = 0.562 m (reasonable)
>
> **Step 3)**   <u>Choose the COMMON SENSE answer:</u>
> Obviously the answer is that 562 mm = <u>0.562 m</u>

Conversion Factors and Metric Units

Example 3:

"If £1 is equal to 1.7 US Dollars, how much is 63 US Dollars in £s?"

> **Step 1)** <u>Find the CONVERSION FACTOR</u>
> In this question the <u>Conversion Factor is</u> obviously <u>1.7</u>
> (When you're changing foreign money it's called the 'Exchange Rate')
>
> **Step 2)** <u>MULTIPLY AND DIVIDE by the conversion factor</u>:
> $$63 \times 1.7 = 107.1 = £107.10$$
> $$63 \div 1.7 = 37.06 = £37.06$$
>
> **Step 3)** <u>Choose the COMMON SENSE answer</u>:
> Not quite so obvious this time, but since 1.7 US Dollars = £1, you're
> clearly going to have <u>fewer</u> pounds than you had Dollars (roughly half).
> In other words, the answer has to be <u>less than</u> 63, so it's <u>£37.06</u>

Example 4:

"A popular item at our local Supplies is 'Froggatt's
Lumpy Sprout Ketchup' (not available in all areas).
The Farmhouse Economy Size is the most popular
and weighs 2400 g. How much is this in kg?"

Gimme
gimme.

> **Step 1)** <u>Conversion Factor = 1000</u>   (simply because 1 kg = 1000 g)
>
> **Step 2)**   2400 × 1000 = 2 400 000 kg   (Uulp..)
>   2400 ÷ 1000 = 2.4 kg   (that's more like it)
>
> **Step 3)** So the answer must be that 2400 g = <u>2.4 kg</u>

Example 5:

"Toby, my pet elephant, weighs 12 tonnes. How much does he weigh in kg?"

> **Step 1)** <u>Conversion Factor = 1000</u>   (as 1 tonne = 1000 kg)
>
> **Step 2)**   12 × 1000 = 12 000 kg   (looks OK)
>   12 ÷ 1000 = 0.012 kg   (that's a pretty light elephant)
>
> **Step 3)** So the answer must be that 12 tonnes = <u>12 000 kg</u>

<u>You don't have the Conversion Factor. I thought it was very karaoke...</u>

What a nice feeling — two lovely pages and just the <u>3 steps</u> of the <u>Conversion Factor method</u> to learn.
If you're reading this and you've still no idea how to find the Conversion Factor — <u>look at all the big colourful
boxes on the last two pages</u>. Not only are they pretty, they'll help you with these...

1) Kevin the Sea-slug was found to weigh 0.16 tonnes. What is this in kg?
2) Froggatt's also do a super-size sarnie. How long is 0.37 m in cm?

Drawing and Measuring

A lot of things you measure have a value which you can never know exactly, no matter how carefully you try and measure them.

Measurements Need to be Rounded Off

Take this slimy grey slug for example (a much smaller relative of Kevin from p34):

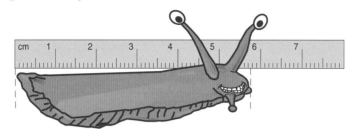

It has a length somewhere between 5cm and 6cm and if you look closer you can even say it's somewhere between 5.7cm and 5.8cm, but you can't really tell any more accurately than that.

So really we only know its length to within 0.1cm. (But let's face it, who needs to know the length of a slimy slug more accurately than that?)

The thing is though that whenever you measure such things as lengths, weights, speeds etc, you always have to take your answer to a certain level of accuracy because you can never get the exact answer.

The simple rule is:

You always round off to the number that it's NEAREST TO

If we take our slimy slug, then to the nearest cm his length is 6cm (rather than 5cm) and to the nearest 0.1cm it's 5.8cm (rather than 5.7).

Possible Error of Half a Unit when Rounding

Whenever a measurement is rounded off to a given UNIT the actual measurement can be anything up to HALF A UNIT bigger or smaller.

EXAMPLES:

1) A room is given as being '9m long to the nearest METRE' — its actual length could be anything from 8.5m up to 9.5m — i.e. HALF A METRE either side of 9m.

2) If it was given as '9.4m, to the nearest 0.2m', then it could be anything from 9.3m up to 9.5m — i.e. 0.1m either side of 9.4m.

3) 'A school has 460 pupils to 2 Sig Fig' (i.e. to the nearest 10) — the actual figure could be anything from 455 up to 464.   — (Why isn't it 465?)

Drawing and Measuring

You might get a question where you need to give the <u>exact value</u> of an angle rather than an estimate. If this happens — <u>DON'T PANIC</u>, just reach for your <u>protractor</u> and follow the advice given below.

Using Protractors

The <u>2 big mistakes</u> that people make with PROTRACTORS:

> 1) <u>Not putting the 0° line at the start position</u>
> 2) <u>Reading from the WRONG SCALE</u>.

These scales won't work...

Two Rules for Getting it Right

1) <u>ALWAYS</u> position the protractor with the <u>base line</u> (0°) along one of the lines as shown here:

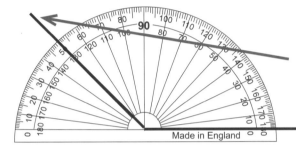

Count in 10° steps from the <u>start line</u> right round to the <u>other one</u> over there.

←Start line

2) <u>COUNT THE ANGLE IN 10° STEPS</u> from the start line right round to the other one.

> <u>DON'T JUST READ A NUMBER OFF THE SCALE</u> — chances are it'll be the <u>WRONG ONE</u> because there are <u>TWO scales to choose from</u>.
>
> The answer here is 130° — NOT 50° — which you will only get right if you start counting 10°, 20°, 30°, 40° etc. from the start line until you reach the other line. You should also <u>estimate</u> it as a check.

... neither will these.

Drawing Angles

You need <u>2 pieces of equipment</u> to draw an accurate angle:

> 1) A protractor
> 2) A ruler

1) Position the <u>protractor</u> with the base line along the start line and <u>count</u> the angle in <u>10° steps</u> (like above).
2) Count up to the number you're after (e.g. 80°) and put a <u>pencil mark</u> there.
3) Then use a <u>ruler</u> to <u>join</u> your mark to the start line — and hey presto, you've drawn an accurate angle.

Use this to draw a <u>pie chart</u> (see p.23):

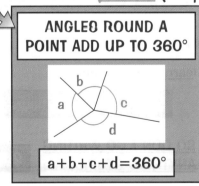

ANGLES ROUND A POINT ADD UP TO 360°

a+b+c+d=360°

Roses are red, tulips are plum, if you were an angle you'd be acute one...

Ho, ho, ho — pretty funny aren't I. Anyway, moving on...
1) x is measured as 2 m to the nearest m. What's the smallest value that x can be?
2) LEARN 2 rules for using protractors.
3) Use a protractor to accurately draw these angles: a) 35° b) 150° c) 80°

Clock Time Questions

 You see <u>24 hour clocks</u> in lots of places so hopefully you're an expert in how to read them. The only thing you might need reminding about is 'am' and 'pm' in the <u>12 hour clock</u>:

`20:23:47`

`08:23:47`

1) am and pm

'am' means '<u>morning</u>'. It runs <u>from 12 midnight to 12 noon</u>.

'pm' means '<u>afternoon</u> and <u>evening</u>'. It runs <u>from 12 noon to 12 midnight</u>.

(though I guess you know that already)

2) Conversions

You'll definitely need to know these very important facts:

> 1 day = 24 hours
> 1 hour = 60 minutes
> 1 minute = 60 seconds

3) Exam questions involving 'time'

There are lots of different questions they can ask involving time but the same <u>GOOD OLD RELIABLE DEPENDABLE METHOD</u> will work wonders on all of them.

"And what is this good old reliable dependable method?", I hear you cry. Well, it's this:

> <u>Take your time</u>, <u>write it down</u>, and <u>split it up</u> into **SHORT EASY STAGES**

EXAMPLE: Find the time taken by a train which sets off at 1325 and arrives at 1910.

<u>WHAT YOU DON'T DO</u> is try to work it all out in your head <u>in one go</u> — this method <u>fails</u> <u>nearly every time</u>. Instead, split it into <u>short easy stages</u> like this:

$$1325 \quad \rightarrow \quad 1400 \quad \rightarrow \quad 1900 \quad \rightarrow \quad 1910$$
$$\text{35 mins} \qquad \text{5 hours} \qquad \text{10 mins}$$

This is a nice safe way of finding the total time from 1325 to 1910:

5 hours + 35 mins + 10 mins = <u>5 hours 45 mins</u>.

4) If you use your Calculator, beware...

Try to avoid using the calculator with time measurements — it's a pain in the neck. You'll get answers in decimals, and you have to convert them into hours and minutes.

So <u>learn this example</u>:

> 2.5 hours = 2 ½ hours = 2 hours and 30 minutes

That sound right? Of course it does.

<u>SO DON'T GO WRITING ANYTHING STUPID</u>, like:

> 2.5 hours = 2 hours and 50 minutes

WRONG WRONG WRONG WRONG!!

BREAKING NEWS: Public panic after warning over calculator use...

You probably know lots of this stuff already. The tips are <u>useful</u> though — so don't just ignore them.

1) What is 1715 in 12 hour clock? (don't forget am/pm)
2) A plane sets off at 10.15 am. The flight lasts 5 hrs 50 mins. What is the arrival time?
3) How many minutes are there in a day? And how many seconds are there in a day?
4) What is 3.5 hours in hours and minutes? What is 5¾ hours in hours and minutes?

Revision Summary for Unit 1 — Part 2

WHAT YOU'RE SUPPOSED TO DO HERE is put all the methods
of the second half of Unit 1 into practice to answer these questions.

1) Work out: a) -3 × -2   b) -4 × 8   c) 12 ÷ -4   d) -20 ÷ -4

2) Claire and James are playing battleships.
Their grids, with their ships shown in grey, are drawn below.
   a) Claire guesses the point (7, 2) on James's grid. James says "miss". Is he cheating?
   b) James guesses (4, 6) on Claire's grid. Has he hit a ship?

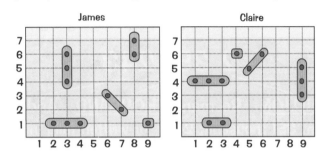

3) Plot these points on a grid: A(1,4), B(-4,2), C(-3,-5), D(5,-6), E(5,0)

4) Say if each of the following are straight line equations or not.
   a) x + 3 = y   b) y + x² = 2   c) y/2 = 1 – 2x   d) y² = x

5) Find the gradient of the straight line that passes
through the points (0, 1) and (3, 10).

6) Sarah has carried out an experiment to find the
rate of photosynthesis at 30 °C. Use her graph to
calculate how much oxygen is produced per minute.

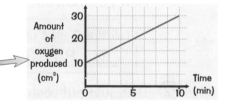

7) These are the sort of numbers you
might get in your calculator display:
   a) 1.2343534   b) 2.9999999   c) 15.534624   d) 12.0833
   Round them off to the nearest whole number.

8) a) Give 246 to the nearest 10   b) Give 860 to the nearest 100

9) How many significant figures have these numbers got?
   a) 12   b) 150   c) 2000   d) 23.4   e) 8500

10) Chris plans to wallpaper a wall that is 4.17 m high and 11.85 m wide.
The wallpaper he wants to use is 60 cm wide and comes in 5 m-long rolls.
How many rolls of wallpaper should he buy?

11) Without using your calculator, estimate the answer to $\dfrac{390}{28 + 12.3}$

12) Kylie is on holiday in South Africa, where £1 = 12.12 rand.
She pays 250 rand to go to a safari park. How much has she spent in pounds?

13) 1 mile = 1.6 km. How many miles is 27 km? Give it to the nearest mile.

14) John's train leaves the station at 1.15 pm. He knows it takes him 25 mins to walk to the
station. What is the latest time he should leave the house?

Ordering Numbers and Place Value

Here's a nice easy page to get you going. You need to be able to:
1) <u>Read big numbers</u>   E.g. how would you say 1 734 564?
2) <u>Write them down</u>   E.g. write '<u>Thirty-two thousand and three</u>' as a number.

Always Look at *Big Numbers* in Groups of *Three*

1) Always start from the extreme <u>right-hand side</u> of the number →
2) Moving <u>left</u>, ←, put a space in <u>every 3 digits</u> to break it up into <u>groups of 3</u>.
3) Now going <u>right</u>, →, <u>read each group of three</u> as a separate number and add 'million' and 'thousand' on for the first two groups (assuming 3 groups in all).

2 351 243

So many **MILLION**   So many **THOUSAND**   And the rest
(i.e. 2 million, 351 thousand, 243) or written fully in words:
Two million, three hundred and fifty-one thousand, two hundred and forty-three.

Putting Numbers in *Order of Size*

Example: 12   84   623   32   486   4563   75   2143

① It may not be exactly difficult, but it's still best to do it in two steps.
First put them into groups, the ones with fewest digits first:

> (all the 2-digit ones,   then all the 3-digit ones,   then all the 4-digit ones etc.)
> |12 84 32 75| |623 486| |4563   2143|

② Then just put each separate group in order of size:

> |12 32 75 84| |486 623| |2143 4563|

> For decimals, do the whole-number bit first before looking at what's after the point.
> With numbers between 0 and 1, first group them by the number of 0s at the start.
> The group with the most 0s at the start comes first, just like this:
>
> (those with 2 initial 0s,   then those with 1 initial 0,   then those with no initial 0s.)
> |0.0026 0.007| |0.03 0.098| |0.14 0.531 0.7|
>
> Once they're in groups, just order them by comparing the first <u>non-zero</u> digits.
> (If the first digits are the same, look at the next digit along instead.)

Hint: Don't call numbers big or small to their face — they're very sensitive...

There's nothing too tricky about putting numbers into order of size — just remember the <u>tips above</u>.
In fact, you might even find it <u>strangely satisfying</u>. A bit like alphabetising your CD collection.

1) Write these numbers in words: a) 1 234 531   b) 23 456   c) 2415   d) 3402   e) 203 412
2) Write this down as a number: Fifty-six thousand, four hundred and twenty-one
3) Put these numbers in order of size: 23   493   87   1029   3004   345   9
4) Write these numbers in ascending order: 0.37 0.008 0.307 0.1 0.09 0.2

Multiplying by 10, 100, etc

You really should know the stuff on this page because:
a) it's <u>nice 'n simple</u>, and   b) they're likely to <u>test you on it</u> in the Exam.

1) <u>To Multiply Any Number by 10</u>

Move the Decimal Point <u>ONE</u> place <u>BIGGER</u> and if it's needed, <u>ADD A ZERO</u> on the end.

<u>Examples:</u>
23.6 × 10 = <u>2 3 6</u>

345 × 10 = <u>3 4 5 0</u>

45.678 × 10 = <u>4 5 6 .7 8</u>

2) <u>To Multiply Any Number by 100</u>

Move the Decimal Point <u>TWO</u> places <u>BIGGER</u> and <u>ADD ZEROS</u> if necessary.

<u>Examples:</u>
296.5 × 100 = <u>2 9 6 5 0</u>

34 × 100 = <u>3 4 0 0</u>

2.543 × 100 = <u>2 5 4 . 3</u>

3) <u>To Multiply by 1000 or 10 000</u>, the same rule applies:

Move the Decimal Point so many places <u>BIGGER</u> and <u>ADD ZEROS</u> if necessary.

<u>Examples:</u>
341 × 1000 = <u>3 4 1 0 0 0</u>

2.3542 × 10 000 = <u>2 3 5 4 2</u>

You always <u>move</u> the <u>DECIMAL POINT</u> this much:
<u>1 place for 10</u>,   <u>2 places for 100</u>,
<u>3 places for 1000</u>,   <u>4 for 10 000</u>   etc.

4) <u>To Multiply by Numbers like 20, 300, 8000 etc.</u>

<u>MULTIPLY</u> by <u>2</u> or <u>3</u> or <u>8</u> etc. <u>FIRST</u>, then move the Decimal Point so many places <u>BIGGER</u> ( ) according to how many noughts there are.

<u>Example:</u>
To find 234 × 200,   <u>first multiply by 2</u>   234 × 2 = 468,
                      then <u>move the DP 2 places</u>   = <u>46800</u>

<u>Adding zeros when they're not needed? Tut, tut, noughty, noughty...</u>

Just <u>four multiplying methods</u> to learn here — nothing too strenuous. For a bit of a workout, try these:
1) Work out   a) 12.3 × 100   b) 345 × 10   c) 9.65 × 1000
2) Work out   a) 2.4 × 20   b) 1.5 × 300   c) 60 × 3000

Dividing by 10, 100, etc

This is <u>pretty easy</u> stuff too. Just <u>make sure you know it</u> — that's all.

1) To Divide Any Number by 10

Move the Decimal Point **ONE** place **SMALLER** and if it's needed, **REMOVE ZEROS** after the decimal point.

<u>Examples:</u>

$23.6 \div 10 = \underline{2 \,.\, 3\, 6}$

$34 \div 10 = \underline{3 \,.\, 4}$

$45.678 \div 10 = \underline{4 \,.\, 5\, 6\, 7\, 8}$

2) To Divide Any Number by 100

Move the Decimal Point **TWO** places **SMALLER** and **REMOVE ZEROS** after the decimal point.

<u>Examples:</u>

$296.5 \div 100 = \underline{2 \,.\, 9\, 6\, 5}$

$340 \div 100 = \underline{3 \,.\, 4}$

$2543 \div 100 = \underline{2\, 5 \,.\, 4\, 3}$

3) To Divide by 1000 or 10 000, the same rule applies:

Move the Decimal Point so many places **SMALLER** and **REMOVE ZEROS** after the decimal point.

<u>Examples:</u>

$341 \div 1000 = \underline{0 \,.\, 3\, 4\, 1}$

$23\,500 \div 10\,000 = \underline{2 \,.\, 3\, 5}$

You always <u>move</u> the <u>DECIMAL POINT</u> this much:

<u>1 place for 10,</u>   <u>2 places for 100,</u>

<u>3 places for 1000,</u>   <u>4 for 10 000</u>   etc.

4) To Divide by Numbers like 40, 300, 7000 etc.

<u>DIVIDE</u> by <u>4</u> or <u>3</u> or <u>7</u> etc. <u>FIRST</u>, then move the Decimal Point so many places <u>SMALLER</u> (i.e. to the left ↶).

<u>Example:</u>

To find $960 \div 300$,   <u>first divide by 3</u> $960 \div 3 = 320$,

then <u>move the DP 2 places smaller</u> $= \underline{3.2}$

With love to guide us, nothing can divide us...

... a great man once said. In other news, knowing how to divide by <u>multiples of 10</u> will be very handy.

1) Work out   a) $2.45 \div 10$ b) $654.2 \div 100$ c) $3.08 \div 1000$

2) Work out   a) $32 \div 20$ b) $360 \div 30$ c) $4000 \div 800$

Addition and Subtraction

You need to know how to do these without a calculator.
The method is the same for whole numbers or decimals.

Adding

1) Line up the <u>units</u> columns of each number.

2) Add up the columns from <u>right to left</u>.

3) <u>Carry over</u> any spare tens to the next column.

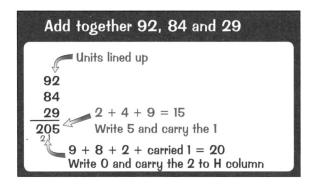

Add together 92, 84 and 29

Units lined up

```
  92
  84
  29
 205
```

2 + 4 + 9 = 15
Write 5 and carry the 1

9 + 8 + 2 + carried 1 = 20
Write 0 and carry the 2 to H column

Subtracting

1) Line up the <u>units</u> columns of each number.

2) Working <u>right to left</u>, subtract the <u>bottom</u> number from the <u>top</u> number.

3) If the top number is <u>smaller</u> than the bottom number, <u>borrow</u> 10 from the left.

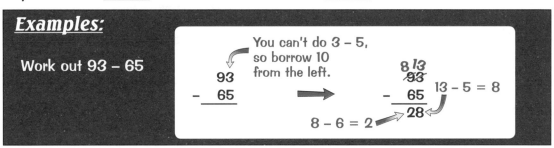

Examples:

Work out 93 – 65

You can't do 3 – 5, so borrow 10 from the left.

```
  93          8 13
           /9̶3̶
- 65       -  65
            28
```

13 – 5 = 8

8 – 6 = 2

And With Decimals...

The <u>method's just the same</u>, but start instead by lining up the <u>decimal points</u>.

Work out 3.74 + 24.2 + 0.6

Decimal points lined up

```
   3.74
  24.2
   0.6
  28.54
```

3 + 4 + 0 + the 1 carried over = 8

7 + 2 + 6 = 15
Write 5 and carry the 1

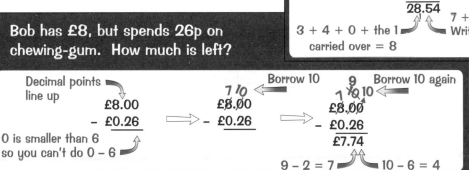

Bob has £8, but spends 26p on chewing-gum. How much is left?

Decimal points line up

```
  £8.00
- £0.26
```

0 is smaller than 6 so you can't do 0 – 6

Borrow 10

```
   7 10
  £8.0̶0
- £0.26
```

Borrow 10 again

```
     9
   1 0̶ 10
  £8.0̶0
- £0.26
  £7.74
```

9 – 2 = 7   10 – 6 = 4

Don't forget to include the units in your answer.

Addition and Subtraction — All it needs is a bit of give and take...

Decimals are <u>just as easy</u> to add and subtract — make sure everything <u>lines up</u> and you'll be fine.

1) When Ric was 10 he was 142 cm tall. Since then he has grown 29 cm.

   a) How tall is he now? b) How much more must he grow before he is 190 cm tall?

2) I have 3 litres of water and drink 1.28 litres. How much is left?

Unit 2 — Number Algebra and Geometry 1

Multiplying Without a Calculator

You need to be really happy doing multiplications <u>without</u> a calculator — you'll definitely need to do it in your exam. So make sure you learn the methods on this page...

Multiplying Whole Numbers

There are lots of methods you can use for this. Two of the popular ones are shown below. Just make sure <u>you can do it</u> using whichever method <u>you prefer</u>...

The Traditional Method:

Split it into separate multiplications, and then add up the results in columns (right to left).

```
      46
  ×   27
  ───────
     322  ── This is 7 × 46
     920  ── This is 20 × 46
  ───────
    1242
```

The 'Gelosia' Method:

Arrange the calculation like below and do 4 easy multiplications to fill up the grid...

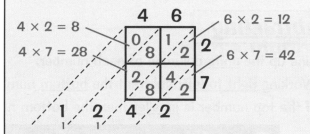

$4 \times 2 = 8$
$4 \times 7 = 28$
$6 \times 2 = 12$
$6 \times 7 = 42$

Then just add up along the diagonals (going right to left) to get the answer.

Answer in both cases: $46 \times 27 = 1242$

Multiplying Decimals

OK, this is a little more tricky — so you'll just have to make sure you <u>learn</u> it.

1) To start with, <u>forget</u> about the decimal points and do the multiplication using <u>whole numbers</u>.
   (E.g. for 1.2 × 3.45 you'd do 12 × 345.)

2) Now <u>count</u> the total number of digits after the <u>decimal points</u> in the original numbers.
   (E.g. 1.2 and 3.45 — so that's 3 digits after the decimal point.)

3) Make the answer have the same number of decimal places.

EXAMPLE: "Work out 4.6 × 2.7"

1) We know that 46 × 27 = 1242 ('cos we've just worked it out)

2) 4.6 × 2.7 has 2 digits after the decimal points

3) So the answer is <u>12.42</u>

Dividing Without a Calculator

OK, time for dividing now. Just remember, if you don't learn these basic methods, you'll find yourself in real trouble in the exam...

Dividing Whole Numbers

EXAMPLE: "What is 896 ÷ 8?"

$$\begin{array}{r} 1 \\ 8\overline{)896} \end{array}$$

8 into 8 goes once.

$$\begin{array}{r} 11 \\ 8\overline{)89\,{}^16} \end{array}$$

8 into 9 goes once,
carry the remainder of 1.

$$\begin{array}{r} 112 \\ 8\overline{)89\,{}^16} \end{array}$$

8 into 16 goes twice,
so 896 ÷ 8 = 112.

Dividing with Decimals

EXAMPLE: "What is 52.8 ÷ 3?"

Just set it out like the one we've just done but put the decimal point in the answer right above the one in the question...

$$\begin{array}{r} 1 \\ 3\overline{)5\,{}^22.8} \end{array}$$

3 into 5 goes once,
carry the remainder of 2.

$$\begin{array}{r} 17. \\ 3\overline{)5\,{}^22.{}^18} \end{array}$$

3 into 22 goes 7 times,
carry the remainder of 1.

$$\begin{array}{r} 17.6 \\ 3\overline{)5\,{}^22.{}^18} \end{array}$$

3 into 18 goes 6 times exactly.
So 52.8 ÷ 3 = 17.6.

EXAMPLE: "What is 36.6 ÷ 0.12?"

The trick with one like this is to remember it's a fraction: $\dfrac{36.6}{0.12}$

Now you can get rid of the decimals by multiplying the top and bottom by 100 (turning it into an equivalent fraction): $\dfrac{36.6}{0.12} = \dfrac{3660}{12}$

It's now a lovely decimal-free division that you know how to solve:

$$12\overline{)3660}$$

12 into 3 won't go
so carry the 3.

$$\begin{array}{r} 3 \\ 12\overline{)3\,{}^366\,0} \end{array}$$

12 into 36 goes 3
times exactly.

$$\begin{array}{r} 30 \\ 12\overline{)3660} \end{array}$$

12 into 6 won't go
so carry the 6.

$$\begin{array}{r} 305 \\ 12\overline{)366\,{}^60} \end{array}$$

12 into 60 goes 5 times
so 36.6 ÷ 0.12 = 305.

Sums without calculators — less painful than standing on a plug barefoot...

Hmm, lots of info to take in there — it's really important that you learn all the methods on these two pages though. Have another read if you're still a bit unsure. Then try all of these without a calculator:

1) 28 × 12
2) 56 × 11
3) 104 × 8
4) 96 ÷ 8
5) 242 ÷ 2
6) 84 ÷ 7
7) 3.2 × 56
8) 0.6 × 10.2
9) 5.5 × 10.2
10) 33.6 ÷ 0.6
11) 45 ÷ 1.5
12) 84.6 ÷ 0.12

Prime Numbers

There's one more special number sequence you need to know about — the Prime Numbers...

1) Basically, PRIME Numbers Don't Divide by Anything

...and that's the best way to think of them. (Strictly, they divide by themselves and 1).
So Prime Numbers are all the numbers that DON'T come up in Times Tables:

| 2 | 3 | 5 | 7 | 11 | 13 | 17 | 19 | 23 | 29 | 31 | 37 | ... |

As you can see, they're an awkward-looking bunch (that's because they don't divide by anything!).
E.g.

The only numbers that multiply to give 7 are 1×7
The only numbers that multiply to give 31 are 1×31

In fact the only way to get ANY PRIME NUMBER is: $1 \times$ ITSELF

2) They End in 1, 3, 7 or 9

1) 1 is NOT a prime number.
2) The first four prime numbers are 2, 3, 5 and 7.
3) Prime numbers end in 1, 3, 7 or 9 (2 and 5 are the only exceptions to this rule).
4) But NOT ALL numbers ending in 1, 3, 7 or 9 are primes, as shown here:
(Only the circled ones are primes)

②	③	⑤	⑦
⑪	⑬	⑰	⑲
21	㉓	27	㉙
㉛	33	㊲	39
㊶	㊸	㊼	49
51	㊵	57	㊾
㊽	63	㊻	69

3) How to FIND Prime Numbers – a very simple method

1) Since all primes (above 5) end in 1, 3, 7, or 9, then to find a prime number between say, 70 and 80, the only possibilities are: 71, 73, 77 and 79

2) Now, to find which of them ACTUALLY ARE primes you only need to divide each one by 3 and 7. If it doesn't divide exactly by either 3 or 7 then it's a prime.
(This simple rule using just 3 and 7 is true for checking primes up to 120)

So, to find the primes between 70 and 80, just try dividing 71, 73, 77 and 79 by 3 and 7:

$71 \div 3 = 23.667$ $71 \div 7 = 10.143$ so 71 IS a prime number
(because it ends in 1, 3, 7 or 9 and it doesn't divide by 3 or 7)

$73 \div 3 = 24.333$ $73 \div 7 = 10.429$ so 73 IS a prime number

$79 \div 3 = 26.333$ $79 \div 7 = 11.286$ so 79 IS a prime number

$77 \div 3 = 25.667$ BUT: $77 \div 7 = 11$ — 11 is a whole number (or 'integer'),
so 77 is NOT a prime, because it divides by 7.

Two is the oddest prime of all — it's the only one that's even...

Learn all three sections above, then cover the page and write down everything you've just learned.
1) Write down the first 15 prime numbers (without looking them up).
2) Using the above method, find all the prime numbers between 90 and 110.

Multiples, Factors and Prime Factors

Hmm, the words above look <u>important</u>. Panic ye not, explanations and examples are on their way...

Multiples

The <u>MULTIPLES</u> of a number are simply its <u>TIMES TABLE</u>:

E.g. the <u>multiples of 13</u> are: 13   26   39   52   65   78   91   104 ...

Factors

The <u>FACTORS</u> of a number are all the numbers that <u>DIVIDE INTO IT</u>.   There's a special way to find them:

EXAMPLE 1

"Find <u>ALL</u> the factors of 24".

Start off with 1× the number itself, then try 2×, then 3× and so on, listing the pairs in rows like this.

Try each one in turn and put a dash if it doesn't divide exactly. Eventually, when you get a number <u>repeated</u>, you <u>stop</u>.

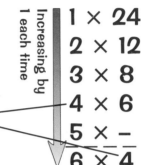

Increasing by 1 each time

1×24
2×12
3×8
4×6
$5 \times -$
6×4

So the <u>FACTORS OF 24</u> are
<u>1, 2, 3, 4, 6, 8, 12, 24</u>

This method guarantees you find them <u>ALL</u> — but <u>don't forget 1 and 24!</u>

EXAMPLE 2

"Find the factors of 64".

<u>Check each one in turn</u>, to see if it divides or not. Use your calculator when you can, if you're not totally confident.

1×64
2×32
$3 \times -$
4×16
$5 \times -$
$6 \times -$
$7 \times -$
8×8

So the <u>FACTORS OF 64</u> are
<u>1, 2, 4, 8, 16, 32, 64</u>

The 8 has <u>repeated</u> so <u>stop here</u>.

Finding Prime Factors — The Factor Tree

<u>Any number</u> can be broken down into a <u>string</u> of PRIME NUMBERS all <u>multiplied</u> together — this is called '<u>Expressing it as a product of prime factors</u>'. To be honest it's pretty tedious – but it's in the Exam, <u>and it's not difficult so long as you know what it is</u>.

The mildly entertaining '<u>Factor Tree</u>' method is best, where you start at the top and split your number off into factors as shown. Each time you get a prime, you <u>ring it</u> and you finally end up with <u>all the prime factors</u>, which you can then arrange <u>in order</u>.

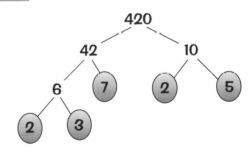

So, 'As a <u>product of prime factors</u>',
$420 = \underline{2 \times 2 \times 3 \times 5 \times 7}$

"I run marathons, cycle everyday..." — quote from a factor in his prime...

Learn what <u>multiples</u>, <u>factors</u> and <u>prime factors</u> are, and <u>how to find them</u>. Turn over and write it down.
1)   List the first 10 multiples of 7, and the first 10 multiples of 11.
2)   List <u>all</u> the factors of 36 and <u>all</u> the factors of 84.
3)   Express as a product of prime factors: a) 990   b) 160.

LCM and HCF

Two big fancy names but don't be put off — they're both really easy.

LCM — 'Lowest Common Multiple'

'Lowest Common Multiple' — sure, it sounds kind of complicated but all it means is this:

> **The SMALLEST number that will DIVIDE BY ALL the numbers in question.**

Method
1) LIST the MULTIPLES of ALL the numbers.
2) Find the SMALLEST one that's in ALL the lists.
3) Easy peasy innit.

> **Example** Find the lowest common multiple (LCM) of 6 and 7.
>
> Multiples of 6 are: 6, 12, 18, 24, 30, 36, (42,) 48, 54, 60, 66, ...
> Multiples of 7 are: 7, 14, 21, 28, 35, (42,) 49, 56, 63, 70, 77, ...
>
> So the lowest common multiple (LCM) of 6 and 7 is 42. Told you it was easy.

HCF — 'Highest Common Factor'

'Highest Common Factor' — all it means is this:

> **The BIGGEST number that will DIVIDE INTO ALL the numbers in question.**

Method
1) LIST the FACTORS of all the numbers.
2) Find the BIGGEST one that's in ALL the lists.
3) Easy peasy innit.

Use the method on p.47 to work out the factors.

> **Example** Find the highest common factor (HCF) of 36, 54, and 72.
>
> Factors of 36 are: 1, 2, 3, 4, 6, 9, 12, (18,) 36
> Factors of 54 are: 1, 2, 3, 6, 9, (18,) 27, 54
> Factors of 72 are: 1, 2, 3, 4, 6, 8, 9, 12, (18,) 24, 36, 72
>
> So the highest common factor (HCF) of 36, 54 and 72 is 18. Told you it was easy.

Just take care listing the factors — make sure you use the proper method (as shown on the previous page) or you'll miss one and blow the whole thing out of the water.

Highest common revision related injury — papercuts...

Make sure you're happy with what LCM and HCF are, and how to find them. Then have a go at these chaps:
1) List the first 10 multiples of 8, and the first 10 multiples of 9.   What's their LCM?
2) List all the factors of 56 and all the factors of 104.   What's their HCF?
3) What's the Lowest Common Multiple of 7 and 9?
4) What's the Highest Common Factor of 36 and 84?

Powers

Right. <u>LEARN THIS PAGE</u>, then <u>PEEL ME SOME GRAPES</u> and <u>IRON MY SHIRTS</u>.
Sorry, I think the power's gone to my head...

Powers are a very Useful Shorthand

$$2\times2\times2\times2\times2\times2\times2 = 2^7 \text{ ('two to the power 7')}$$
$$7\times7 = 7^2 \text{ ('7 squared')}$$
$$6\times6\times6\times6\times6 = 6^5 \text{ ('Six to the power 5')}$$
$$4\times4\times4 = 4^3 \text{ ('four cubed')}$$

That bit is easy to remember. Unfortunately, there are <u>SIX SPECIAL RULES</u> for powers that
are not quite so easy, but <u>you do need to know them for the Exam</u>:

The Five Rules   The <u>first two</u> only work for powers of the <u>SAME NUMBER</u>.

1) When <u>MULTIPLYING</u>, you <u>ADD the powers</u>.

e.g. $3^4 \times 3^6 = 3^{4+6} = 3^{10}$ $8^3 \times 8^5 = 8^{3+5} = 8^8$

2) When <u>DIVIDING</u>, you <u>SUBTRACT the powers</u>.

e.g. $5^4 \div 5^2 = 5^{4-2} = 5^2$ $12^8/12^3 = 12^{8-3} = 12^5$

3) When <u>RAISING</u> one power to another, you <u>MULTIPLY the powers</u>.

e.g. $(3^2)^4 = 3^{2\times4} = 3^8,$ $(5^4)^6 = 5^{24}$

4) $X^1 - X,$ ANYTHING TO THE POWER 1 is just ITSELF

e.g. $3^1 = 3,$ $6 \times 6^3 = 6^4,$ $4^3 \div 4^2 = 4^{3-2} = 4^1 = 4$

5) $1^x = 1,$ 1 TO ANY POWER is still just 1

e.g. $1^{23} = 1$ $1^{89} = 1$ $1^2 = 1$ $1^{1012} = 1$

"I've got the power! oh, oh, oh, oh..." Oh no, I'm feeling kinda 90s...

Some say you should learn the <u>Five Rules</u> for Powers. Then <u>turn over</u> and <u>write it all down</u>.
Well, I say keep trying until you can do it, then cover the page and apply the rules to <u>simplify</u> these.
1) a) $3^2 \times 3^6$ b) $4^3 \div 4^2$ c) $(8^3)^4$ d) $(3^2 \times 3^3 \times 1^6) / 3^5$ e) $7^3 \times 7 \times 7^2$
2) a) $5^2 \times 5^7 \times 5^3$ b) $1^3 \times 5^0 \times 6^2$ c) $(2^5 \times 2 \times 2^6) \div (2^3 \times 2^4)$

Square Roots and Cube Roots

Take a deep breath, and get ready to tackle this page. Good luck with it, I'll be rootin' for ya...

Square Roots

'Squared' means 'times by itself' : $P^2 = P \times P$
— SQUARE ROOT is the reverse process.

The best way to think of it is this:

> **'Square Root' means**
> **'What Number Times by Itself gives...'**

Example: 'Find the square root of 49'   (i.e. 'Find $\sqrt{49}$')
To do this you should say "what number times by itself gives... 49?"
And the answer of course is 7.

Square Roots can be Positive or Negative

When you take the square root of a number, the answer can actually be positive or negative... you always have a positive and negative version of the same number.

E.g.
> $x^2 = 4$ gives $x = \pm\sqrt{4} = +2$ or -2

To understand why, look at what happens when you work backwards
by squaring the answers: $2^2 = 2 \times 2 = 4$ but also $(-2)^2 = (-2) \times (-2) = 4$

Cube Roots

'Cubed' means 'times by itself three times' : $T^3 = T \times T \times T$
— CUBE ROOT is the reverse process.

> **'Cube Root' means 'What Number**
> **Times by Itself THREE TIMES gives...'**

Well, strictly there are only two × signs, but you know what I mean.

Example: "Find the cube root of 64"   (i.e 'Find $\sqrt[3]{64}$')

You should say "What number times by itself three times gives... 64?"
And after a few guesses, the answer is 4.
(Note — unlike square roots, there's only ever one answer.)

"Cue brute", that's what I call Charley when I play him at snooker...

LEARN the 2 statements in the blue boxes and the methods for finding the roots.
Then turn the page and write it all down.
1) Find: a) $\sqrt{81}$ b) $\sqrt[3]{27}$
If you got only one answer for a) what is the other answer?
2) a) If $g^2 = 36$, find g.   b) If $b^3 = 125$, find b.   c) If $4 \times r^2 = 36$, find r.

Unit 2 — Number Algebra and Geometry 1

Fractions

This page covers all the essentials for dealing with fractions <u>without your calculator</u>.
You need to make sure that you can do <u>everything</u> explained here. Every last smidgen.

Equivalent Fractions

Equivalent fractions are fractions that are <u>equal in value</u>, even though they look different.

Starting with any fraction you like, you can make up a list of equivalent fractions by simply <u>MULTIPLYING top and bottom</u> by the <u>SAME NUMBER</u> each time:

$$\frac{1}{2} \overset{\times 3}{\underset{\times 3}{=}} \frac{3}{6} \qquad \frac{3}{4} \overset{\times 5}{\underset{\times 5}{=}} \frac{15}{20} \qquad \frac{1}{5} \overset{\times 100}{\underset{\times 100}{=}} \frac{100}{500}$$

Cancelling Down

Going the other way, you will sometimes need to <u>simplify</u> a fraction by '<u>cancelling down</u>' — which only means <u>DIVIDING top and bottom</u> by the <u>SAME NUMBER</u>, until you can't divide them any more:

$$\frac{3}{15} \overset{\div 3}{\underset{\div 3}{=}} \frac{1}{5} \qquad \frac{22}{33} \overset{\div 11}{\underset{\div 11}{=}} \frac{2}{3}$$

Ordering Fractions — Make the Bottom Numbers the Same

E.g. Put these fractions in <u>ascending</u> order of size: $\frac{8}{3}, \frac{6}{4}, \frac{12}{5}$

① First, to find the new denominator, just find the <u>LCM</u> (see p48) of the denominators:

② Then change each fraction to an <u>equivalent</u> one that's over the new number:

③ Now they're <u>easy</u> to write in order:

LCM of 3, 4 and 5 is <u>60</u>

$$\frac{8}{3} \overset{\times 20}{\underset{\times 20}{=}} \frac{160}{60} \qquad \frac{6}{4} \overset{\times 15}{\underset{\times 15}{=}} \frac{90}{60} \qquad \frac{12}{5} \overset{\times 12}{\underset{\times 12}{=}} \frac{144}{60}$$

$$\frac{90}{60}, \frac{144}{60}, \frac{160}{60} \text{ or } \frac{6}{4}, \frac{12}{5}, \frac{8}{3}.$$

Finding a Fraction of Something — just Multiply

<u>Multiply</u> the 'something' by the <u>TOP</u> of the fraction, then <u>divide</u> it by the <u>BOTTOM</u>:

$$\frac{9}{20} \text{ of } £360 = \{(9) \times £360\} \div (20) = \frac{£3240}{20} = £162$$

$$\text{or: } \frac{9}{20} \text{ of } £360 = \frac{9}{1} \times £360 \times \frac{1}{20} = £162$$

LIGHTS... CAMERA... fffrrrACTION...

1) Reduce these fractions to their simplest form: a) $\frac{30}{36}$ b) $\frac{18}{27}$ 2) Order these fractions: $\frac{11}{15}, \frac{3}{5}, \frac{2}{3}$

3) Find $\frac{2}{5}$ of 550. b) What's $\frac{7}{8}$ of £2?

Fractions

Here are some more ways to cope with fraction calculations without your beloved calculator. (For some tricks on doing fractions with your calculator, see p.3.)

1) Multiplying — easy

Multiply top and bottom separately:

$$\frac{3}{5} \times \frac{4}{7} = \frac{3 \times 4}{5 \times 7} = \frac{12}{35}$$

I'll see myself out.

2) Dividing — quite easy

Turn the 2nd fraction UPSIDE DOWN and then multiply:

$$\frac{3}{4} \div \frac{1}{3} = \frac{3}{4} \times \frac{3}{1} = \frac{3 \times 3}{4 \times 1} = \frac{9}{4}$$

3) Adding, Subtracting — fraught

Add or subtract TOP LINES ONLY but only if the denominators (bottom numbers) are the same.

(If they're not, you have to make them the same — see previous page).

$$\frac{2}{6} + \frac{1}{6} = \frac{3}{6}$$

$$\frac{5}{7} - \frac{3}{7} = \frac{2}{7}$$

4) Dealing with Mixed Numbers

There's only one way to deal with calculations involving mixed numbers (that's things like $3\frac{1}{3}$):

1) change them to 'normal' fractions
2) then you can calculate with them as usual.

Don't try to do them any other way, because you'll probably get it wrong.

$$3\frac{2}{3} \times 7\frac{3}{4} = \frac{11}{3} \times \frac{31}{4}$$

$2 + (3 \times 3)$

$3 + (7 \times 4)$

$$= \frac{341}{12}$$

You might end up with an improper fraction like this, where the top number is larger than the bottom number.

To turn this back into a mixed number without using the calculator, you'll have to do the division ($341 \div 12$ in this case) to work out the number of times the top number goes into the bottom number, and if there's a remainder.

E.g. $341 \div 12 = 28$ r 5, so $\frac{341}{12} = 28\frac{5}{12}$

The number of times 341 divides by 12

The remainder stays as the top number in the fraction.

No fractions were harmed in the making of this page...

Now you've learnt those five useful tips, it's time to have a go at these below — without a calculator.

1) a) $\frac{3}{8} \times \frac{5}{12}$ b) $\frac{4}{5} \div \frac{7}{8}$ c) $\frac{3}{4} + \frac{2}{5}$ d) $\frac{2}{5} - \frac{3}{8}$ e) $4\frac{1}{9} + 2\frac{2}{27}$

Fractions and Recurring Decimals

You might think that a decimal is just a decimal. But oh no — things get a lot more juicy than that...

Decimals can be Recurring or Terminating

1) <u>Recurring</u> decimals have a <u>pattern</u> of numbers which repeats forever, e.g. $\frac{1}{3}$ is the decimal 0.333333... It can be several digits that repeat. You could have, for instance: 0.143143143...

2) <u>Terminating</u> decimals are <u>finite</u>, e.g $\frac{1}{20}$ is the decimal 0.05.

The <u>denominator</u> (bottom number) of a fraction, tells you if it'll be a <u>recurring</u> or <u>terminating</u> <u>decimal</u> when you convert it. Fractions where the denominator has <u>prime factors</u> of <u>only 2 or 5</u> will give <u>terminating decimals</u>. All <u>other fractions</u> will give <u>recurring decimals</u>.

See P47 for more on prime factors.

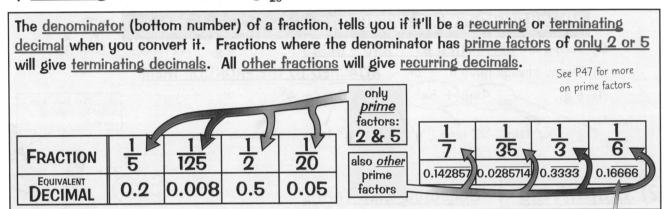

FRACTION	$\frac{1}{5}$	$\frac{1}{125}$	$\frac{1}{2}$	$\frac{1}{20}$	$\frac{1}{7}$	$\frac{1}{35}$	$\frac{1}{3}$	$\frac{1}{6}$
EQUIVALENT DECIMAL	0.2	0.008	0.5	0.05	$0.\overline{142857}$	$0.0\overline{285714}$	$0.\overline{3333}$	$0.1\overline{6666}$

only *prime* factors: **2 & 5**

also *other* prime factors

You can write recurring decimals like this — the line goes above the repeating part of the decimal.

Turning Recurring Decimals into Fractions

There's two ways to do it: 1) by <u>UNDERSTANDING</u>   2) by just <u>LEARNING THE RESULT</u>.

The Understanding Method:

Find the <u>length</u> of the <u>repeating sequence</u> and <u>multiply</u> by 10, 100, 1000, 10 000 or whatever to move it all up past the decimal point by <u>one full repeated lump</u>:

E.g. 0.234234234... × 1000 = 234.234234...

<u>Subtract the original number</u>, r, from the new one (which in this case is 1000r)

i.e. 1000r − r = 234.234234... − 0.234234... giving: 999r = 234

Then just <u>DIVIDE</u> to leave r: $r = \frac{234}{999}$, and cancel if possible: $r = \frac{26}{111}$

The 'Just Learning The Result' Method:

The fraction always has the repeating unit on the top and the same number of nines on the bottom — easy as that. Look at these and marvel at the elegant simplicity of it.

$0.4444444... = \frac{4}{9}$ $0.34343434... = \frac{34}{99}$ $0.124124124... = \frac{124}{999}$ $0.14561456... = \frac{1456}{9999}$

Always check if it will <u>CANCEL DOWN</u> of course, e.g. $0.363636... = \frac{36}{99} = \frac{4}{11}$.

Not fractions again — they're like a recurring nightmare...

Learn how to tell whether a fraction will be a <u>terminating or recurring decimal</u>, and both the <u>methods above</u>. Then turn over and write it all down. Now, try and answer these beauties...

1) Express 0.142857142857... as a fraction.

2) Without cheating, say if these fractions will give recurring or terminating decimals: a) $\frac{3}{8}$ b) $\frac{9}{280}$ c) $\frac{7}{250}$

Algebra

Algebra really terrifies so many people. But honestly, it's not that bad. You've just got to make sure you <u>understand and learn</u> these <u>basic rules</u> for dealing with algebraic expressions. After that, all it needs is practice, practice, practice... and a little love.

1) Terms

Before you can do anything else, you <u>MUST</u> understand what a <u>TERM</u> is:

1) <u>A TERM IS A COLLECTION OF NUMBERS, LETTERS AND BRACKETS, ALL MULTIPLIED/DIVIDED TOGETHER.</u>

2) Terms are <u>SEPARATED BY + AND − SIGNS</u>   e.g. $4x^2 − 3py − 5 + 3p$ Terms

3) Terms always have a + or − <u>ATTACHED TO THE FRONT OF THEM</u>

4) e.g. $(− 4xy)$ $(+ 5x^2)$ $(− 2y)$ $(+6y^2)$ $(+ 4)$

Invisible + sign

'xy' term   'x²' term   'y' term   'y²' term   'number' term

Like... Yeah love. I err... collect like terms err... and stuff...

This date isn't going well...

2) Simplifying

'Collecting Like Terms'

<u>EXAMPLE:</u> "Simplify $2x − 4 + 5x + 6$"

$(2x)(−4)(+5x)(+ 6)$ = $(+2x)(+5x)(−4)(+6)$

x-terms   number terms   = $7x$ $+2$ = $\underline{7x + 2}$

1) <u>Put bubbles round each term,</u> — be sure you <u>capture the +/− sign IN FRONT</u> of each.

2) Then you can <u>move the bubbles into the best order</u> so that <u>LIKE TERMS</u> are together.

3) '<u>LIKE TERMS</u>' have exactly the same combination of letters, e.g. 'x-terms' or 'xy-terms'.

4) <u>Combine LIKE TERMS</u> using the <u>NUMBER LINE</u> (not the other rule for negative numbers).

3) Multiplying out Brackets

Learn these 4 rules:

1) The thing <u>OUTSIDE</u> the brackets <u>multiplies each separate term INSIDE the brackets.</u>

2) When letters are <u>multiplied together</u>, they are just <u>written next to each other</u>, e.g. pq

3) Remember, $R \times R = R^2$, and TY^2 means $T \times Y \times Y$, whilst $(TY)^2$ means $T \times T \times Y \times Y$.

4) Remember <u>a minus outside the bracket REVERSES ALL THE SIGNS when you multiply.</u>

<u>EXAMPLE:</u>   1) $3(2x + 5) = 6x + 15$ 2) $4p(3r − 2t) = 12pr − 8pt$

3) $− 4(3p^2 − 7q^3) = − 12p^2 + 28q^3$ ——— (note both signs have been <u>reversed</u> — Rule 4)

Go forth and multiply out brackets...

<u>Learn</u> all the <u>key facts</u> on this page, then have a go at these questions to see how well you've got it.

1) Simplify: a) $5x + 3y − 4 − 2y − x$ b) $3x + 2 + 5xy + 6x − 7$

         c) $2x + 3x^2 + 5y^2 + 3x$ d) $3y − 6xy + 3y + 2yx$

2) Expand: a) $2(x − 2)$ b) $x(5 + x)$ c) $y(y + x)$ d) $3y(2x − 6)$

Algebra

4) Factorising — putting brackets in

This is the exact reverse of multiplying-out brackets. Here's the method to follow:

> 1) Take out the biggest NUMBER that goes into all the terms.
> 2) For each letter in turn, take out the highest power (e.g. x, x^2 etc) that will go into EVERY term.
> 3) Open the brackets and fill in all the bits needed to reproduce each term.

EXAMPLE: Factorise $15x^4y + 20x^2y^3z - 35x^3yz^2$

ANSWER: $5x^2y(3x^2 + 4y^2z - 7xz^2)$

Biggest number that'll divide into 15, 20 and 35

Highest powers of x and y that will go into all three terms

z wasn't in ALL terms so it can't come out as a common factor

REMEMBER: 1) The bits taken out and put at the front are the common factors.
2) The bits inside the brackets are what's needed to get back to the original terms if you were to multiply the brackets out again.

Just Follow the Method

In GCSE Maths, you're often asked to use formulas like this one: $F = \dfrac{9}{5}C + 32$
It looks scary — but this topic is a lot easier than you think...

Example: Use the formula above to convert 15 °C from Celsius (C) into Fahrenheit (F).

Method:

1) Write out the Formula   e.g $F = \dfrac{9}{5}C + 32$

2) Write it again, directly underneath, but substituting numbers for letters on the RHS. (Right Hand Side) $F = \dfrac{9}{5}15 + 32$

3) Work it out IN STAGES.
Use BODMAS to work things out IN THE RIGHT ORDER.
WRITE DOWN values for each bit as you go along.
$F = 27 + 32$
$= 59$
$F = 59°$

4) DO NOT attempt to do it all in one go on your calculator.
That ridiculous method fails at least 50% of the time.

> If you don't follow this STRICT METHOD you'll just keep getting them wrong — it's as simple as that.

It could be worse. Probably. If you think about it. I'm sure it could...

The techniques on these two pages really are the nuts n' bolts of algebra. There's no getting out of it, you'll have to knuckle down and learn everything on these pages inside out. Then have a crack at these:

1) Factorise: a) $5xy + 15x$ b) $5a - 7ab$ c) $12xy + 6y - 36y^2$
2) Use the formula $a = 2c^2 - 6$ to find a, when $c = 9$.

Making Formulas from Words

These can seem a bit confusing but they're not as bad as they look, once you know the "tricks of the trade", as it were. There are two main types.

Type 1

In this type there are <u>instructions about what to do with a number</u> and you have to write it as a <u>formula</u>. The only things they're likely to want you to do in the formula are:

1) Multiply x   2) Divide x   3) Square x (x^2)   4) Add or subtract a number

Example   "To find y, multiply x by three and then subtract four"

Answer: Start with x $\rightarrow$ 3x $\rightarrow$ 3x − 4   so <u>y = 3x − 4</u>

Times it by 3   Subtract 4   (not too gruelling, is it?)

Type 2

This is a bit harder. <u>You have to make up a formula</u> by putting in letters like 'C' for '<u>cost</u>' or 'n' for '<u>number of something-or-others</u>'. Although it may look confusing, the formulas always turn out to be <u>REALLY SIMPLE</u>, so make sure you give it a go.

Example 1:   Froggatt's deep-fry 'CHOCCO-BURGERS' (chocolate-covered beef burgers — not available in all areas) cost 58 pence each. Write a formula for the total cost, T, of buying n 'CHOCCO-BURGERS' at 58p each.

Answer: T stands for the total cost

n stands for the number of 'CHOCCO-BURGERS'

In words the formula is: Total Cost = Number of 'CHOCCO-BURGERS' × 58p

Putting the letters in: T = n × 58   or to write it better: <u>T = 58n</u>

Example 2:   Horse repellant costs £1.50 for a 150 ml bottle. Write a formula for the total cost, T, of buying horse repellant, where b is the number of bottles.

Answer: T stands for the total cost

b stands for the number of bottles

In words the formula is: Total Cost = Number of bottles × £1.50

Putting the letters in: T = b × 1.5   or to write it better: <u>T = 1.5b</u>

I'm so impressed with this page that words fail me...

Nope. I got nothin'. Best just do these questions:

1) The value of y is found by taking x, multiplying it by five and then subtracting three. Write down a formula for y in terms of x.

2) One of Froggatt's main competitors is "Sleigh-deer foods", who produce some tasty reindeer kebabs which cost 95p a skewer.
Write a formula for the total cost C pence of buying n kebabs.

Special Number Sequences

You need to know all the types of number sequence on this page.
And as you'll find out, they're each _special_ in their very own way. Bless.

EVEN Numbers all Divide by 2

| 2 4 6 8 10 12 14 16 18 20 ... |

All EVEN numbers END in 0, 2, 4, 6 or 8
e.g. 200, 342, 576, 94

ODD Numbers Don't Divide by 2

| 1 3 5 7 9 11 13 15 17 19 21 ... |

All ODD numbers END in 1, 3, 5, 7 or 9
e.g. 301, 95, 807, 43

SQUARE Numbers:

They're called SQUARE NUMBERS because
they're like the areas of this pattern of squares:

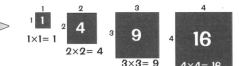

(1×1) (2×2) (3×3) (4×4) (5×5) (6×6) (7×7) (8×8) (9×9) (10×10) (11×11) (12×12) (13×13) (14×14) (15×15)

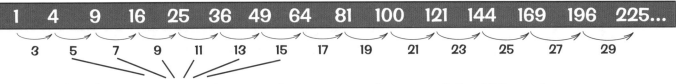

| 1 4 9 16 25 36 49 64 81 100 121 144 169 196 225... |

3 5 7 9 11 13 15 17 19 21 23 25 27 29

Note that the DIFFERENCES between the square numbers are all the ODD numbers.

CUBE Numbers:

They're called CUBE NUMBERS because they're
like the volumes of this pattern of cubes.

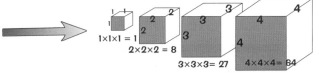

(1×1×1) (2×2×2) (3×3×3) (4×4×4) (5×5×5) (6×6×6) (7×7×7) (8×8×8) (9×9×9) (10×10×10)...

| 1 8 27 64 125 216 343 512 729 1000... |

POWERS:

Powers are 'numbers multiplied by themselves so many times'
'Two to the power three' = 2^3 = 2 × 2 × 2 = 8

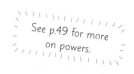

See p.49 for more on powers.

Here are the first few POWERS OF 2:

| 2 4 8 16 32... |

2^1=2 2^2=4 2^3=8 2^4=16 etc...

... and the first POWERS OF 10 (even easier):

| 10 100 1000 10 000 100 000... |

10^1=10 10^2=100 10^3=1000 etc...

What do you do if your cube numbers are sad? Tell them they're special...

1) Cover up the page and then write down the first 15 numbers in all six sequences.
2) From this list of numbers: 23, 45, 56, 81, 25, 97, 134, 156, 125, 36, 64
   write down: a) all the even numbers   b) all the odd numbers   c) all the square numbers
   d) all the cube numbers   e) all the powers of 2 or 10

Unit 2 — Number Algebra and Geometry 1

Number Patterns and Sequences

There are five different types of <u>number sequences</u> you could get in the exam, each as pretty as the last. They're not difficult — <u>AS LONG AS YOU WRITE WHAT'S HAPPENING IN EACH GAP.</u>

1) 'Add or Subtract the Same Number'

The SECRET is to <u>write the differences in the gaps</u> between each pair of numbers:

E.g.   2   5   8   11   14   ...   30   24   18   12   ...
                +3   +3   +3   +3   +3   - 6   -6   -6   -6

> <u>The RULE:</u>   'Add 3 to the <u>previous term</u>'   'Subtract 6 from the <u>previous term</u>'

2) 'Add or Subtract a Changing Number'

Again, <u>WRITE THE CHANGE IN THE GAPS</u>, as shown here:

E.g.   8   11   15   20   26   ...   or   53   43   34   26   19   ...
             +3   +4   +5   +6   +7   -10   -9   -8   -7   -6

> <u>The RULE:</u> 'Add 1 <u>extra</u> each time to the <u>previous term</u>'   'Subtract 1 <u>less</u> from the <u>previous term</u>'

3) Multiply by the Same Number each Time

This type have a common <u>MULTIPLIER</u> linking each pair of numbers:

E.g.   5   10   20   40   ...   2   6   18   54   ...
             ×2   ×2   ×2   ×2   ×3   ×3   ×3   ×3

> <u>The RULE:</u>   'Multiply the <u>previous term</u> by 2'   'Multiply the <u>previous term</u> by 3'

4) Divide by the Same Number each Time

This type have the same <u>DIVIDER</u> between each pair of numbers:

E.g.   400   200   100   50   ...   40 000   4000   400   40   ...
             ÷2   ÷2   ÷2   ÷2   ÷10   ÷10   ÷10   ÷10

> <u>The RULE:</u>   'Divide the <u>previous term</u> by 2'   'Divide the <u>previous term</u> by 10'

5) Add the Previous Two Terms

This type of sequence works by adding the last two numbers to get the next one.

E.g.   1   1   2   3   5   8   13   ...   2   4   6   10   16   ...
                  1+1 1+2 2+3 3+5 5+8 8+13   2+4   4+6 6+10 10+16

> <u>The RULE:</u>   'Add the previous two terms'

Number Patterns and Sequences

'State the rule for extending the pattern'

This is what a lot of Exam questions end up asking for and it's easy enough
so long as you remember this:

> ALWAYS say what you do to the **PREVIOUS TERM** to get the next term.

All the number sequences on the previous page have the rule for extending the pattern
written in the box underneath them.   Notice that they all refer to the previous term.

Finding the nth number:

You could be asked in the Exam to 'give an expression for the nth number in the
sequence.' You'll only have to do this for a 'type 1' sequence (where the same number
is added or subtracted). It's not that difficult because there's a simple formula:

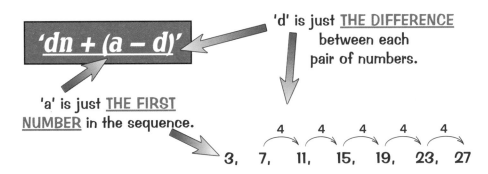

'dn + (a − d)'

'd' is just THE DIFFERENCE
between each
pair of numbers.

'a' is just THE FIRST
NUMBER in the sequence.

$$3, \quad 7, \quad 11, \quad 15, \quad 19, \quad 23, \quad 27$$
(differences of 4 between each)

To get the nth term, you just find the values of 'a' and 'd' from the sequence
and stick them in the formula. You don't replace n though — that wants to
stay as n. Of course you have to learn the formula, but life is like that.

> **Example:** "Find the nth number of this sequence: 5, 8, 11, 14 ...."
>
> 1) The formula is dn + (a − d)
> 2) The first number is 5, so a = 5. The differences are 3 so d = 3
> 3) Putting these in the formula gives: 3n + (5 − 3) = 3n + 2
>
> So the nth number for this sequence is given by: '3n + 2'

Identifying numbers not in a sequence:

> **Example:** "Is 13 in the sequence 2n + 1 where n is a whole number?"
> Treat it like an equation where you want to find n: 2n + 1 = 13
>   2n = 12
>
> So yes, 13 is in the sequence.   n = 6

Look, if I've told you n times, I've told you n + 1 times — learn this page...

LEARN the 5 types of number patterns and the formula for finding the nth number and Bob's your uncle.

1) Find the next two numbers in each of these sequences, and say in words what the rule is for extending each one:
a) 2, 5, 9, 14 ....   b) 2, 20, 200 ....   c) 64, 32, 16, 8 ...

2) Find the expression for the nth number in this sequence: 7, 9, 11, 13

Midpoint of a Line Segment

Man, that's one scary sounding title, but don't let it fool you.
When you get down to it, finding the midpoint is just a spot of <u>adding</u> and <u>dividing by two</u>.

The 'Midpoint' is just the Middle of the Line

The '<u>MIDPOINT OF A LINE SEGMENT</u>' is the <u>POINT THAT'S BANG IN THE MIDDLE</u> of it.

(Not exactly rocket science, is it...)

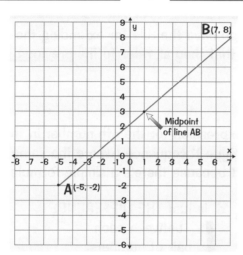
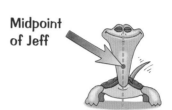

Midpoint of Jeff

Find the Coordinates of a Midpoint

The only thing you really need to know about midpoints is how to find the coordinates of one.

And it's pretty easy. The x-coordinate of the midpoint is the average of the
x-coordinates of the end points — and the same goes for the y-coordinates.

<u>EXAMPLE</u>: "A and B have coordinates (2, 1) and (6, 3)
Find the midpoint of the line AB."

ALWAYS START BY DRAWING A GRAPH

Then follow these <u>THREE EASY STEPS</u>...

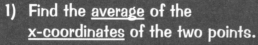

1) Find the <u>average</u> of the <u>x-coordinates</u> of the two points.

2) Find the <u>average</u> of the <u>y-coordinates</u> of the two points.

3) Plonk them in <u>brackets</u>.

Average of x-coordinates
$= (2 + 6) \div 2 = \underline{4}$

Average of y-coordinates
$= (1 + 3) \div 2 = \underline{2}$

Plonk them in brackets
(x-coordinate first): $(\underline{4}, \underline{2})$

To find the midpoint — average, average, plonk

<u>Learn the 3 easy steps</u> for finding midpoints. Close the book and <u>write them down</u>.
Plot these points on some graph paper: A(1, 4), B(5, 6), C(3, 2), D(7, 0).
1) Draw a line between points A and B and find the midpoint of the line AB.
2) Draw a line between points C and D and find the midpoint of line CD.

Drawing Straight-Line Graphs

Strap on a beret, grab a pencil and let's get arty (well, graphy at least) — it's graph drawing time.

1) Doing the Table of Values

1) What you're likely to get in the Exam is an equation such as
"$y = x + 3$", or "$y = 3x + 2$" and a half-finished table of values:

> **Example:** "Complete this table of values, using the equation $y = 2x - 7$"
>
> | x | -2 | 0 | 2 | 4 | 6 |
> |---|----|---|---|---|---|
> | y | -11 | | -3 | | |

2) Put each x-value into the equation and work out the corresponding y-values.

E.g. <u>For x = 0</u>, $y = 2x - 7 = (2 \times 0) - 7 = 0 - 7 = \underline{-7}$, etc...

...until you get this:

x	-2	0	2	4	6
y	-11	-7	-3	1	5

2) Plotting The Points and Drawing The Graph

1) <u>PLOT EACH PAIR</u> of x- and y- values from the table as a point on the graph.

2) Do it very <u>CAREFULLY</u> — and don't mix up the x- and y-values. (See P.26)

3) The points will always form <u>A DEAD STRAIGHT LINE</u>.

<u>NEVER</u> let one point drag your line off in some ridiculous direction. You <u>never get SPIKES – only MISTAKES</u>.

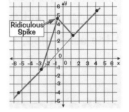

4) If one point does look a bit wacky, check 2 things:
   – the y-value you worked out in the table
   – that you've plotted it properly!

Continuing the Example from part 1):

"Use your table of values to plot the graph of $y = 2x - 7$"

Simple — plot each point carefully, then you should be able to draw a nice <u>STRAIGHT LINE</u> through all the points.

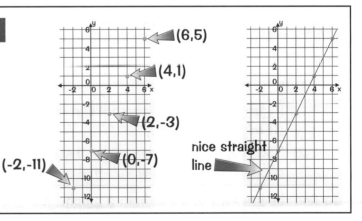

Careful plotting — the key to perfect straight lines and world domination...

... mwah ha ha ha. Learn this page, then have a go at the questions below.

1) <u>Complete this table of values</u> for the equation: $y = x - 2$

x	-4	-2	-1	0	1	2	4
y	-6			-2			

2) Then <u>plot the points on graph paper and draw the graph</u>.

Straight-Line Graphs — y = mx + c

$y = mx + c$ is the general equation for a straight-line graph, and you need to remember:

'm' is equal to the __GRADIENT__ of the graph

'c' is the value __WHERE IT CROSSES THE Y-AXIS__ and is called the __Y-INTERCEPT__.

1) Drawing a Straight Line using "y = mx + c"

The main thing is being able to identify 'm' and 'c' and knowing what to do with them:
BUT WATCH OUT — people often mix up 'm' and 'c', especially with say, '$y = 5 + 2x$'
__REMEMBER__: 'm' is the number __IN FRONT OF X__ and 'c' is the number __ON ITS OWN__.

Method

1) Get the __equation__ into the form '$y = mx + c$'.
2) __Identify__ 'm' and 'c' carefully.
3) Put a __dot__ on the __y-axis__ at the value of c.
4) Then go along one unit and up or down by the value of m and __make another dot__.
5) Repeat the same 'step' in __both directions__ as shown:
6) Finally __check__ that the gradient __LOOKS RIGHT__.

START HERE

$y = 2x + 1$

m = +2 so it's UP 2 units

ALWAYS along ONE Unit →

1) __The graph shows the process for the equation '$y = 2x + 1$':__
   'c' = 1, so put a first dot at $y = 1$ on the y-axis.
2) Go along 1 unit → and then up by 2 because 'm' = +2.
3) Repeat the same step, $1 \to 2$ in __both__ directions. (i.e. $1 \leftarrow 2 \downarrow$ the other way)
4) CHECK: __a gradient of +2 should be quite steep and uphill left to right__ — which it is.

2) Finding the Gradient from the Equation...

All you need to do is __identify the 'm'__ part of the equation and then you've found your gradient. But it's tricky when you find an equation written in a funny way, so make sure it's written in the '$y = mx + c$' form.

__THIS IS EASY__:
1) __Rearrange__ the equation so it's in the '$y = mx + c$' form. (It might be already.)
2) Now __read__ the value for 'm' — that's the __gradient__. If there's a minus in front of the 'm', that's part of the gradient too.

Example:

$3x + y = 2$

$y = -3x + 2$

The gradient is -3.

To find the gradient of a line __from a graph__, you need to check out p.28.

Remember y = mx + c — it'll keep you on the straight and narrow...

That, and remembering the __METHOD__ for __drawing a line__ and __finding the gradient__.
Once you think you've got it, have a go at the questions below.
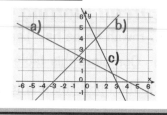
1) Using '$y = mx + c$' draw the graphs of $y = x - 3$ and $y = 4 - 2x$.
2) Using '$y = mx + c$' find the equations of these 3 graphs.
3) The equation $y = 25 - 3x$ produces a straight line, but what is its gradient?

Unit 2 — Number Algebra and Geometry 1

More Graphs

Yay, just what you wanted to see — some more graphs...

Travel Graphs

1) A <u>TRAVEL GRAPH</u> is always <u>DISTANCE</u> (↑) against <u>TIME</u> (→)

2) <u>FLAT SECTIONS</u> are where it's <u>STOPPED</u>.

3) The <u>STEEPER</u> the graph the <u>FASTER</u> it's going.

4) The graph <u>GOING UP</u> means it's travelling <u>AWAY</u>. The graph <u>COMING DOWN</u> means it's <u>COMING BACK AGAIN</u>.

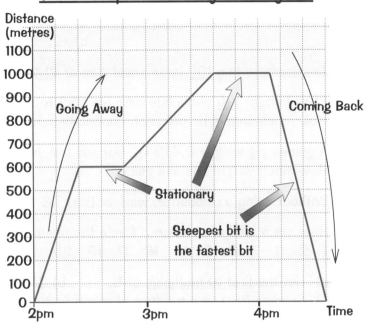

Travel Graph for a Very Tired cyclist

Going Away

Coming Back

Stationary

Steepest bit is the fastest bit

Curved Line Graphs

Sometimes the data you want to plot won't produce nice straight lines, because some situations are represented by <u>curves</u>. An example is a graph of a <u>cyclist slowing down</u>...

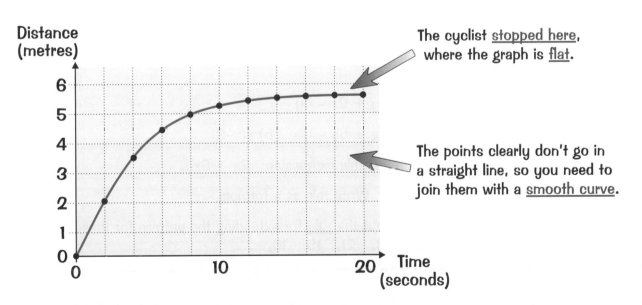

The cyclist <u>stopped here</u>, where the graph is <u>flat</u>.

The points clearly don't go in a straight line, so you need to join them with a <u>smooth curve</u>.

I had a great joke for this space, but it was too graphic...

Travel graphs can be confusing, so take the time to understand them. Then have a go at these questions.

1) On a travel graph, what does it mean when the gradient of the line is negative?

2) If you were plotting a travel graph of a spacecraft launching and the first 5 minutes of the journey, should you use a curved line graph?

Revision Summary for Unit 2 — Part 1

Now you've got to TEST YOUR KNOWLEDGE by writing brilliant answers to these questions on all the stuff you've covered so far in Unit 2.

1) Write this number out in words: 21 306 515

2) Put these numbers in order of size: a) 23 6534 123 2200 2 132 789 45
   b) -2,   4,   0,   -7,   -6,   10,   8,   5

3) Jan needs to buy 100 large envelopes at £1.20 each. How much money does she need?

4) Chris bought 100 chocolate bars for £32 to sell in the school tuck shop.
   How much should he sell each chocolate bar for to make his money back?

5) A guinea pig weighs 0.472 kg, but she weighed only 0.324 kg two months ago.
   How much weight has she gained?

6) Without using a calculator, work out: a) 16×91 b) 29×11 c) 6.3×14 d) $132 \div 11$

7) Here are a load of numbers. Circle the ones which are prime numbers:
   1 2 3 7 8 9 14 16 17 19 20 25 30 60 61 88 99

8) a) List the first 10 multiples of 6.   b) List all the factors of 68.
   c) Express 280 as a product of prime factors.

9) Find the lowest common multiple (LCM) of 9 and 10.

10) What's the highest common factor (HCF) of 48 and 72?

11) Work out the value of: a) 6^4 b) 7^5 c) 4 squared   d) 12^5 e) $5^3 \times 4^7$ f) 8 cubed

12) Find all possible answers of a) $\sqrt{256}$ b) $\sqrt[3]{216}$.

13) Work out without a calculator: a) $\frac{4}{6} \times 4\frac{2}{5}$ b) $\frac{25}{6} \div \frac{8}{3}$ c) $\frac{5}{8} + \frac{9}{4}$ d) $\frac{2}{3} - \frac{1}{7}$

14) Write down whether each of these fractions will convert to a recurring or terminating decimal:
   a) $\frac{18}{25}$ b) $\frac{69}{200}$ c) $\frac{4}{7}$ d) $\frac{27}{11}$

15) Simplify the expression: $3x + 4y + 2x - 4y$

16) Expand these expressions: a) $4(3g + 5h - 1)$ b) $x(x-6)$

17) Factorise (take out common factors) this expression: $2x + 6xy$.

18) 'To find y you double x and add 4.' Write this as a formula.

19) Find the next two terms and work out the rule for extending the pattern for these sequences:
   a) 3, 7, 11, 15, ...   b) 36, 28, 21, 15, 10, ...

20) Work out the expression for the nth number in this sequence: 1, 5, 9, 13, ...

21) Plot the points (-6, -3) and (4, 7) on a grid. Find the coordinates of the midpoint.

22) Complete this table of values for the equation $y = x + 1$ and plot the graph of the equation:

23) State the gradient of $y = 200 + 6x$.

24) What does the steepness of a distance-time graph show?

x	-4	-2	0	2	4
y	-3				

Angles

Angles aren't that bad — you just have to <u>learn</u> them, that's all. And sometimes give them sweets.

1) Estimating Angles

The secret here is to <u>KNOW THESE FOUR SPECIAL ANGLES</u> as <u>reference points</u>.
Then you can **COMPARE** any other angle to them.

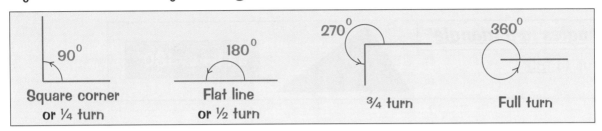

| 90^0 | 180^0 | 270^0 | 360^0 |
| Square corner or ¼ turn | Flat line or ½ turn | ¾ turn | Full turn |

EXAMPLE: Estimate the size of these three angles A, B and C:

If you <u>compare each angle</u> to the reference angles of 90°, 180° and 270° you can easily estimate that:

<u>A = 70°</u>, <u>B = 110°</u>, <u>C = 260°</u>

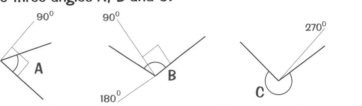

Acute Angles

<u>SHARP POINTY ONES</u>
(less than 90°)

Obtuse Angles

<u>FLATTER-LOOKING ONES</u>
(between 90° and 180°)

Reflex Angles

<u>ONES THAT BEND BACK
ON THEMSELVES</u>
(more than 180°)

Right Angles

<u>SQUARE CORNERS</u>
(exactly 90°)

When two lines meet at 90° they are said to be <u>PERPENDICULAR</u> to each other.

2) Three Letter Angle Notation

The best way to say which angle you're talking about in a diagram is by using <u>THREE</u> letters.
For example in the diagram, <u>angle ACB = 25°</u>.

1) The <u>MIDDLE LETTER</u> is <u>where the angle is</u>.
2) The <u>OTHER TWO LETTERS</u> tell you <u>WHICH TWO LINES</u> enclose the angle.

(Not drawn to scale.)

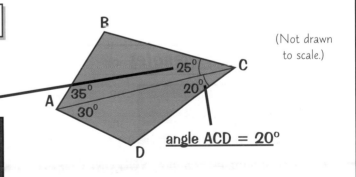

angle ACD = 20°

Marks for guessing the answer — sounds like my kind of topic...

OK, so you won't actually get any marks just for guessing — you need to make a good guess.
Better practise then...

1) Estimate these angles: a)   b)   c)    d)

Unit 2 — Number Algebra and Geometry 1

Angles — The Rules

Rules, rules, rules. Gotta love 'em. And even if you don't, you gotta learn 'em. Try these for size:

6 Simple Rules — that's all:

If you know them <u>ALL</u> — <u>THOROUGHLY</u>, you at least have a fighting chance of working out problems with lines and angles. If you don't — you've no chance.

1) Angles in a triangle

Add up to <u>180°</u>.

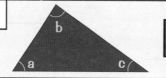

$$a+b+c=180°$$

2) Angles on a straight line

Add up to <u>180°</u>.

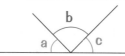

$$a+b+c=180°$$

3) Angles in a 4-sided shape

(a '<u>Quadrilateral</u>')

Add up to <u>360°</u>.

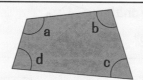

$$a+b+c+d=360°$$

4) Angles round a point

Add up to <u>360°</u>.

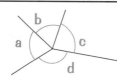

$$a+b+c+d=360°$$

5) Exterior Angle of Triangle

Exterior Angle of triangle $=$ sum of Opposite Interior angles

i.e. $a+b=d$

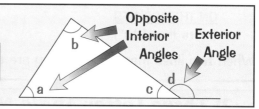

Opposite Interior Angles

Exterior Angle

6) Isosceles triangles

**<u>2 sides</u> the same
<u>2 angles</u> the same**

These dashes indicate two sides the same length

In an isosceles triangle, <u>YOU ONLY NEED TO KNOW ONE ANGLE</u> to be able to find the other two, which is <u>very useful IF YOU REMEMBER IT</u>.

a)

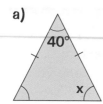

$180° - 40° = 140°$
<u>The two bottom angles are both the same</u> and they must add up to 140°, so each one must be half of 140° (= 70°). So <u>x = 70°</u>.

b)

The <u>two bottom angles must be the same</u>, so $50° + 50° = 100°$.
All the angles add up to 180° so y = 180° - 100° = <u>80°</u>.

Unit 2 — Number Algebra and Geometry 1

Parallel Lines

Up next — parallel lines. These make working out angles <u>even easier</u>. No really, they do...

Angles and Parallel Lines

Whenever one line goes across <u>2 parallel lines</u>, then the two <u>bunches of angles</u> are the <u>same</u>, as shown below:

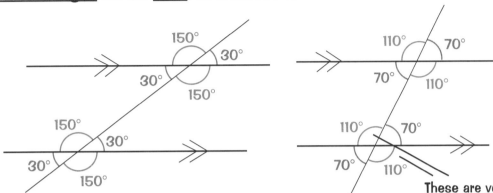

(The arrows mean those 2 lines are parallel)

These are <u>vertically opposite</u> angles.
They're equal to each other.

> Whenever you have <u>TWO PARALLEL LINES</u>...
>
> 1) there are <u>only two different angles</u>: <u>A SMALL ONE</u> and <u>A BIG ONE</u>
>
> 2) and they <u>ALWAYS ADD UP TO 180°</u>. E.g.   30° and 150°   or   70° and 110°

The trickiest bit about parallel lines is <u>SPOTTING THEM IN THE FIRST PLACE</u>
— watch out for these 'Z', 'C', 'U' and 'F' shapes popping up.
They're a dead giveaway that you've got a pair of parallel lines.

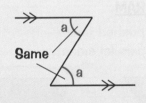

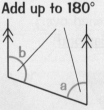

Add up to 180°

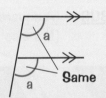

In a Z-shape they're called
"<u>ALTERNATE ANGLES</u>"

If they add up to 180° they're called
"<u>SUPPLEMENTARY ANGLES</u>"

In an F-shape they're called
"<u>CORRESPONDING ANGLES</u>"

Alas, you're expected to learn these three silly names too!

If two lines cross at 90° then you've
got yourself some <u>perpendicular lines</u>.
Mark these beasts by using little squares to show the 90°, like so:

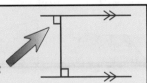

I chose not to choose life. I chose parallel line spotting...

Spotting parallel lines is really, <u>really</u> important, so always have a good look for them.
There are some questions that you <u>won't</u> be able to answer if you miss them.
And I think we'd agree that that's a <u>bad thing</u>.

1) The diagram shown here has one angle given as 60°. Find all the other 7 angles.

2D Shapes

— make sure you know them all.

Three-sided Shapes — Triangles
(just in case you didn't know...)

1) EQUILATERAL Triangle

<u>3 lines</u> of symmetry.
Rotational symmetry <u>order 3</u>

2) RIGHT-ANGLED Triangle

No symmetry unless the angles are <u>45°</u>

3) ISOSCELES Triangle
2 sides equal
2 angles equal

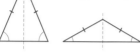

<u>1 line</u> of symmetry.
No rotational symmetry

Four-sided Shapes — Quadrilaterals

1) SQUARE

 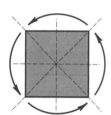

<u>4 lines</u> of symmetry.
Rotational symmetry <u>order 4</u>.

2) RECTANGLE

 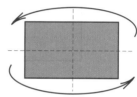

<u>2 lines</u> of symmetry.
Rotational symmetry <u>order 2</u>.

3) RHOMBUS (A square pushed over)
(It's also a <u>diamond</u>)

 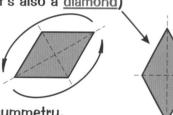

<u>2 lines</u> of symmetry.
Rotational symmetry <u>order 2</u>.

4) PARALLELOGRAM
(A rectangle pushed over — two pairs of parallel sides)

 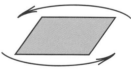

<u>NO lines</u> of symmetry.
Rotational symmetry <u>order 2</u>.

5) TRAPEZIUM (<u>One pair</u> of parallel sides)

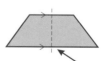 

Only the <u>isosceles trapezium</u> has a <u>line</u> of symmetry.
None have rotational symmetry.

6) KITE

<u>1 line</u> of symmetry.
No rotational symmetry.

Rhombus facts: 4 sides, 2 lines of symmetry, Gemini, peanut allergy...
Learn <u>everything on this page</u>. Then turn over and write down all the details that you can remember. Then try again. It's as simple as that. Then you can play with the kite. Indoors though — it's new.

Unit 2 — Number Algebra and Geometry 1

2D Shapes — Circles

There's a surprising number of <u>circle terms</u> you need to know — don't mix them up. Oh, and it's probably best to have a snack before starting this page. All the talk of <u>pi</u> can make you a bit peckish.

1) Radius and Diameter

The <u>DIAMETER</u> goes <u>right across</u> the circle.
The <u>RADIUS</u> only goes <u>halfway</u> across.

> Remember: the <u>DIAMETER IS EXACTLY DOUBLE THE RADIUS</u>

<u>Examples</u>: If the radius is 4 cm, the diameter is 8 cm,
If the diameter is 24 m, the radius is 12 m.

2) Tangents, Chords, Arcs and the Rest...

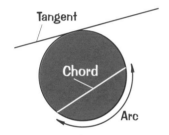

> <u>A TANGENT</u> is a straight line that <u>just touches</u> the <u>outside</u> of the circle.
> <u>A CHORD</u> is a line drawn <u>across the inside</u> of a circle.
> <u>AN ARC</u> is just <u>part of the circumference</u> of the circle.

> <u>A SECTOR</u> is a WEDGE-SHAPED AREA (like a piece of cake) cut right from the centre.
> <u>SEGMENTS</u> are the areas you get when you cut the circle with a chord.

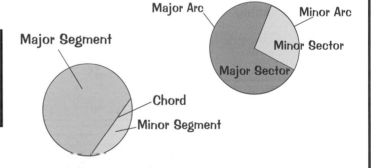

You need a Pair of Compasses to Draw a Circle...

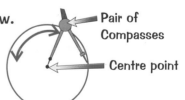

1) Set the compasses' width to the <u>radius</u> of the circle you want to draw.
2) Position the <u>metal point</u> where you want the <u>centre</u> of the circle.
3) <u>Carefully rotate</u> the compasses, drawing a circle as you do.
4) Sit back and <u>admire</u> your lovely circle (before getting a bandage).

Common mistake — a slice of pie is not called a wedgie...

Once again, learn it all, turn over and scribble it down. If you can remember it all, reward yourself with a pie of your choice. Do I want a wedgie? Oh, well, if you're offering it's rude not to...

Unit 2 — Number Algebra and Geometry 1

3D Shapes and Similarity

I was going to make some pop-out <u>3D shapes</u> to put on this page, but I couldn't find the scissors and sticky tape. Sorry. Still, you need to learn it all though — so chin up and learn the page.

Eight Solids To Learn

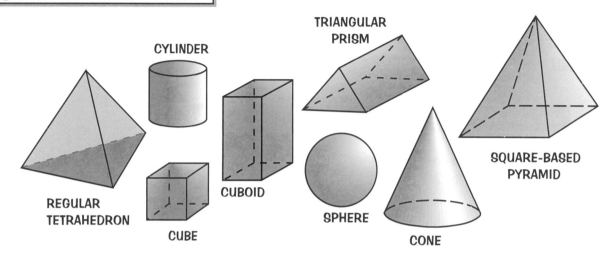

CYLINDER

TRIANGULAR PRISM

REGULAR TETRAHEDRON

CUBOID

CUBE

SPHERE

CONE

SQUARE-BASED PYRAMID

You Need to be Able to Use Isometric Grids

An <u>ISOMETRIC PROJECTION</u> is where a shape is drawn (to scale) from a view at <u>equal angles</u> to all three axes (x, y and z).

Or more simply, it's a drawing like this:

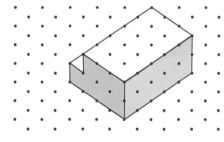

Similar — Same Shape, Different Size

> If two shapes are <u>SIMILAR</u> they are <u>exactly</u> <u>the SAME SHAPE but DIFFERENT SIZES.</u>

<u>SIMILAR</u>: <u>Same</u> shape, <u>different</u> size.

Two similar shapes can be seen as an 'enlargement'.

Remember when you have similar shapes that <u>the angles are always the same</u>.

Well done — you've moved on to solids...

Deep breath in... and out... Cover up the page, then name 8 types of solid object.

1) Draw an isometric projection of your own house.

Symmetry

Symmetry is where a shape or picture can be put in <u>different positions</u> that <u>look exactly the same</u>.

1) Line Symmetry

This is where you can draw a <u>MIRROR LINE</u> (or more than one) across a picture and <u>both sides will fold exactly together</u>.

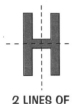

2 LINES OF SYMMETRY   1 LINE OF SYMMETRY   1 LINE OF SYMMETRY   3 LINES OF SYMMETRY   NO LINES OF SYMMETRY   1 LINE OF SYMMETRY

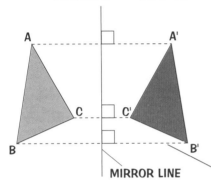

MIRROR LINE

How to Draw a Reflection:

1) Reflect each point one by one.
2) Use a line which crosses the mirror line at 90° and goes <u>EXACTLY</u> the same distance on the other side of the mirror line, as shown.

A line which crosses at 90° is called <u>a perpendicular</u>

2) Rotational Symmetry

This is where you can <u>ROTATE</u> the shape or drawing into different positions that <u>all look exactly the same</u>.

Order 1   Order 2   Order 2   Order 3   Order 4

The <u>ORDER OF ROTATIONAL SYMMETRY</u> is the posh way of saying:
'<u>HOW MANY DIFFERENT POSITIONS LOOK THE SAME</u>'.
E.g. You should say the Z shape above has '<u>Rotational Symmetry order 2</u>'

BUT... when a shape has <u>ONLY 1 POSITION</u> you can <u>either</u> say that it has
'<u>Rotational Symmetry order 1</u>'   <u>or</u> that it has '<u>NO Rotational Symmetry</u>'

Tracing Paper

— this always makes symmetry a lot easier

1) For <u>REFLECTIONS</u>, trace one side of the drawing and the mirror line too.
Then <u>turn the paper over and line up the mirror line</u> in its original position.

2) For <u>ROTATIONS</u>, just swizzle the paper round. It's really good for <u>finding the centre of rotation</u> (by trial and error) as well as the <u>order of rotational symmetry</u>.

3) You can use tracing paper in the <u>EXAM</u> — ask for it, or take your own in.

Mirror mirror on the wall, who's the most symmetrical of all?

Make sure you know the <u>two types of symmetry</u>. Then copy the letters below and mark in all the <u>lines of symmetry</u>. Also, say what the <u>rotational symmetry</u> is for each one.

H   Z   T   N   E   ✗   S

Perimeters

Perimeter is the distance <u>all the way around the outside of a 2D shape</u>. It's pretty straightforward to work out if you use the <u>big blob method</u>. So pay attention — this could be easy marks.

The Perimeter is the Distance Around the Edge of a Shape

To find a <u>PERIMETER</u>, you <u>ADD UP THE LENGTHS OF ALL THE SIDES</u>, but...
<u>THE ONLY RELIABLE WAY</u> to make sure you get <u>all the sides</u> is this:

> 1) <u>PUT A BIG BLOB AT ONE CORNER</u> and then go around the shape.
> 2) <u>WRITE DOWN THE LENGTH OF EVERY SIDE</u> as you go along.
> 3) <u>EVEN SIDES THAT SEEM TO HAVE NO LENGTH GIVEN</u>
>   — you must work them out.
> 4) Keep going until you get back to the <u>BIG BLOB</u>.

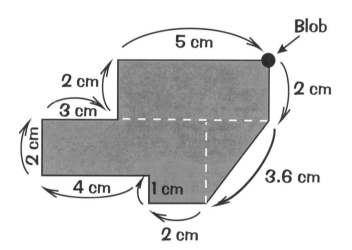

You must choose yourself a blob and it must also choose you. It will then be yours for life.

E.g. 2+3.6+2+1+4+2+3+2+5 = <u>24.6 cm</u>

Yes, I know you think it's <u>yet another fussy method</u>, but believe me, it's so easy to miss a side. You must use good reliable methods for everything — or you'll lose marks willy nilly.

Finding the perimeter of a <u>regular</u> <u>shape</u> is dead easy — you just find the <u>length</u> of <u>one side</u> and <u>multiply</u> it by the <u>number of sides</u>.

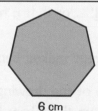

E.g. for this lovely <u>heptagon</u>, each side is 6 cm long. There are <u>7</u> sides, so Perimeter = 6 × 7 = <u>42 cm</u>.

6 cm

RUN — DON'T WALK from... the BIG BLOB...

...no, don't do that really. You need to get friendly with your big blob, and always use him for finding the perimeter of complicated shapes. He should always be willing to help — if not, just feed him a calculator or two and he'll be happy in no time. He's also quite partial to Camembert.

7 cm
6 cm
5 cm
3 cm

1) <u>Turn over and write down</u> what you have learnt.
2) Find the perimeter of the shape shown here.

Areas

First things first — below are four basic area formulas. Best learn these unless you're planning on tipping <u>bucketloads</u> of easy exam marks <u>down the toilet</u>. (If you ARE planning on doing this, you'll need to raise your hand during the exam and ask to go to the bathroom — if they don't disappear on the first flush, <u>pause</u>, and then try again).

You must LEARN these Formulas:

1) RECTANGLE

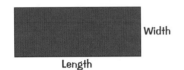
Width
Length

Area of <u>RECTANGLE</u> = length × width

$$A = l \times w$$

2) TRIANGLE

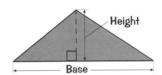
Height
Base

Area of <u>TRIANGLE</u> = ½ × base × vertical height

$$A = \tfrac{1}{2} \times b \times h_v$$

Note that the <u>height</u> must always be the <u>vertical height</u>, not the sloping height.

3) PARALLELOGRAM

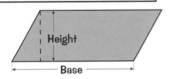
Height
Base

Area of <u>PARALLELOGRAM</u> = base × vertical height

$$A = b \times h_v$$

4) TRAPEZIUM

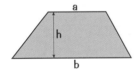
a
h
b

Area of <u>TRAPEZIUM</u> = average of parallel sides × distance between them

$$A = \tfrac{1}{2} \times (a + b) \times h$$

You don't have to remember this one — it'll be on your formula sheet. But make sure you know how to use it.

Areas of More Complicated Shapes

You often have to find the area of <u>strange looking</u> shapes in exam questions. What you always find with these questions is that you can break the shape up into <u>simpler ones</u> that you can deal with.

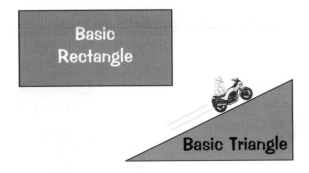
Basic Rectangle
Basic Triangle

1) <u>SPLIT THEM UP</u> into the two basic shapes: <u>RECTANGLE</u> and <u>TRIANGLE</u>
2) Work out the area of each bit <u>SEPARATELY</u>
3) Then <u>ADD THEM ALL TOGETHER</u>

See next page for a lovely example...

Areas

...and here's the lovely example, as promised...

EXAMPLE: Work out the area of the shape shown:

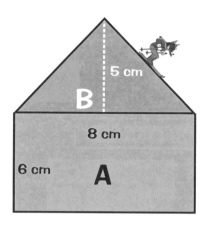

ANSWER:

Shape A is a <u>rectangle</u>:	Shape B is a <u>triangle</u>:
Area = L × W	Area = ½ × b × h
= 8 × 6	= ½ × 8 × 5
= <u>48</u> cm²	= <u>20</u> cm²

<u>TOTAL AREA</u> = 48 + 20 = <u>68</u> cm²

Don't Reach Straight for the Calculator

You might be <u>kidding yourself</u> that it 'takes too long' to write down your working out — but what's so great about getting <u>ZERO MARKS for an easy question</u>?

Compare these two answers to this question:
Find the area of the triangle on the right [3 marks].

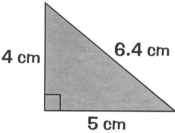

ANSWER 1: ~~[crossed out]~~   <u>20</u>   ✗

<u>ANSWER 1</u> gets <u>NO MARKS AT ALL</u> — 20 is the wrong answer and there's nothing else to give any marks for.

ANSWER 2: A = ½ × B × H ✓
       = ½ × 5 × 4 ✓
       = 10 cm²   ✓

<u>ANSWER 2</u> has <u>3 bits that all get marks</u>, — so even if the answer was wrong it would still get most of the marks!

The thing is though, when you <u>write it down step by step</u>, you can see what you're doing <u>and you won't get it wrong in the first place</u> — try it next time, go on... just for the wild experience.

I need to take my shape to the barbers — it's getting area and area...

Hahaha.... Not amused? OK suit yourself. It's time to <u>memorise the area formulas</u> and learn how to deal with <u>complicated shapes</u>. Then find the areas of these 4 shapes...

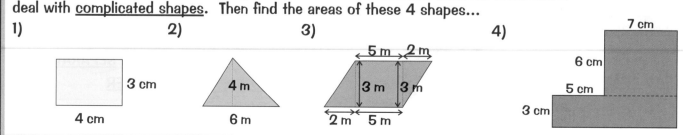

Volume and Surface Area

You need to know what <u>face</u>, <u>edge</u> and <u>vertex</u> mean, and you've come to the right place to find out...

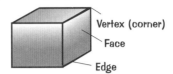

Surface Area

1) <u>SURFACE AREA</u> only applies to solid 3-D objects, and it's simply <u>the total area of all the outer surfaces added together</u>. If you were painting it, it's all the bits you'd paint.

2) There is <u>never a simple formula</u> for surface area — <u>you have to work out the area of each face in turn and then ADD THEM ALL TOGETHER</u>.

EXAMPLE:

Work out the surface area of this shape:

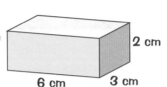

ANSWER:

$(2 \times 3) + (2 \times 3) +$
$(6 \times 3) + (6 \times 3) + (6 \times 2) + (6 \times 2)$
$= 6 + 6 + 18 + 18 + 12 + 12 = \underline{72 \text{ cm}^2}$

VOLUMES — YOU MUST LEARN THESE TOO...

1) Cuboid (rectangular block)

(This is also known as a 'rectangular prism' — see below to understand why.)

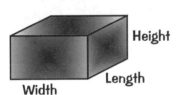

Volume of Cuboid = length × width × height

$$V = l \times w \times h$$

(The other word for volume is <u>CAPACITY</u>)

2) Prism

<u>A PRISM</u> is a solid (3-D) object which is the same shape all the way through — i.e. it has a <u>CONSTANT AREA OF CROSS-SECTION</u>.

Triangular Prism

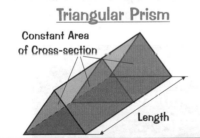

Constant Area of Cross-section

Length

Hexagonal Prism

(a flat one, certainly, but still a prism)

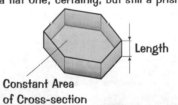

Length

Constant Area of Cross-section

Volume of prism = Cross-sectional Area × length

$$V = A \times l$$

As you can see, the formula for the volume of a prism is <u>very simple</u>.
The <u>difficult</u> part, usually, is <u>finding the area of the cross-section</u>.

Don't make it any more angry — it's already a cross-section...

With things like this, once you've learnt the formula it's a doddle.
You then just need to put the right numbers in and the
answer is yours. All yours. Mwah-ha-ha-ha-haaaaaa.
Find the volume of this prism:

4 cm
3 cm
7 cm
9 cm

Imperial Units

This topic is <u>easy marks</u> — make sure you get them. That sounded a bit like a threat. <u>It wasn't</u>. Honest. I just have poor people skills.

Metric Units

1) <u>Length</u>   mm, cm, m, km
2) <u>Area</u>   mm^2, cm^2, m^2, km^2,
3) <u>Volume</u>   mm^3, cm^3, m^3, litres, ml
4) <u>Weight</u>   g, kg, tonnes
5) <u>Speed</u>   km/h, m/s

MEMORISE THESE KEY FACTS:

1cm = 10mm	1 tonne = 1000kg
1m = 100cm	1 litre = 1000ml
1km = 1000m	1 litre = 1000cm^3
1kg = 1000g	1cm^3 = 1ml

You should recognise some of these from Unit 1.

Imperial Units

1) <u>Length</u>   Inches, feet, yards, miles
2) <u>Area</u>   Square inches, square feet, square yards, square miles
3) <u>Volume</u>   Cubic inches, cubic feet, gallons, pints
4) <u>Weight</u>   ounces, pounds, stones, tons
5) <u>Speed</u>   mph

IMPERIAL UNIT CONVERSIONS:

1 Foot = 12 Inches
1 Yard = 3 Feet
1 Gallon = 8 Pints
1 Stone = 14 Pounds (lbs)
1 Pound = 16 Ounces (oz)

You don't need to know these for the exam, but you should be able to do the conversions.

Metric-Imperial Conversions

<u>YOU NEED TO LEARN THESE</u> — they <u>DON'T</u> promise to give you these in the Exam and if they're feeling mean (as they often are), they won't.

Approximate Conversions

1 kg = 2.2 lbs	1 gallon = 4.5 litres
1 m = 1.1 yard	1 foot = 30cm
1 litre = 1 ¾ Pints	1 metric <u>tonne</u> = 1 imperial <u>ton</u>
1 inch = 2.5 cm	1 mile = 1.6 km
	or 5 miles = 8 km

<u>Imperial units — they're mint...</u>

Learn all the <u>21 Conversions</u> above, then <u>cover</u> the page and see if you can <u>scribble</u> them all down.
1) How many litres is 1500cm^3?
2) A rod is 46 inches long. What is this in feet and inches?
3) a) Roughly how many yards is 200m?   b) How many cm is 6 feet 3 inches?

Unit 2 — Number Algebra and Geometry 1

<u>*Speed*</u>

Formula triangles are <u>extremely useful tools</u> for lots of tricky maths problems.
They're <u>very easy to use</u> and <u>very easy to remember</u>. But don't just take my word for it...

If 3 things are related by a formula that looks either

like this: $A = B \times C$ or like this: $B = \dfrac{A}{C}$

then you can put them into a <u>FORMULA TRIANGLE</u> like this:

1) <u>*First decide where the letters go:*</u>

1) If there are <u>TWO LETTERS MULTIPLIED TOGETHER</u> in the formula
    then they must go <u>ON THE BOTTOM</u> of the Formula Triangle
    (and so <u>the other one</u> must go <u>on the top</u>).

2) If there's <u>ONE THING DIVIDED BY ANOTHER</u> in the formula
    then the one <u>ON TOP OF THE DIVISION</u> goes <u>ON TOP IN THE
    FORMULA TRIANGLE</u> (and so the other two must go <u>on the bottom</u>
           — it doesn't matter which way round).

So the formula '<u>Speed = Distance / Time</u>' fits into a formula triangle like this.

2) <u>*Using the Formula Triangle for Speed = Distance ÷ Time*</u>

This is very common. It probably comes up every single year — and they never give you the
formula. Life isn't all bad though — there's an easy <u>FORMULA TRIANGLE</u>:

Of course you still have to <u>remember the order of the letters</u> in the
triangle ($S^D T$) — but this time we have the word <u>SoDiT</u> to help you.

So if it's a question on speed, distance and time just say: **SOD IT**.

| **EXAMPLE:** | "A car travels 90 miles at 36 miles per hour. How long does it take?" |

  <u>ANSWER</u>: <u>We want to find the TIME</u>, so <u>cover up T</u> in the triangle which leaves D/S,

     so   T = D/S   = Distance ÷ speed   = 90÷36 = <u>2.5 hours</u>

> LEARN THE <u>FORMULA TRIANGLE</u>, AND YOU'LL FIND
> QUESTIONS ON SPEED, DISTANCE AND TIME <u>VERY EASY</u>.

<u>*Formula triangles — it's all a big cover up...*</u>

By now, you should be convinced that formula triangles are the <u>most amazingly useful thing ever</u>.
They'll help make using formulas <u>much easier</u>. The best thing to do is learn the whole page, cover it up
and scribble down everything you can remember. It's a really good way to help you learn everything.

Revision Summary for Unit 2 — Part 2

SEE WHAT YOU KNOW AND SEE WHAT YOU DON'T by answering these questions.
It's all the lovely stuff from the second part of Unit 2. Enjoy...

1) Draw these four special angles:
   a) 90°   b) 180°   c) 270°   d) 360°

2) Most avalanches happen on slopes that are at an angle
   between 15° and 60°. Katie decided to estimate the angle of the
   slope she was on to see whether she was at risk from an avalanche.
   She created a right angled triangle using two ice axes (see diagram).
   Do you think Katie is at risk from an avalanche?

slope

3) What sort of triangle is this?
   Work out angles X and Y in the diagram:

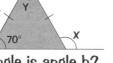

4) If angle a in this diagram is 50°, what angle is angle b?

5) Sharon is making some sample birthday cards for a stationery company.
   She wants to fold each card along a line of symmetry, so it folds exactly together.
   Draw all the lines of symmetry for each of the card designs.
   a)   b)   c)   d)

6) Draw a circle and then show on it a tangent, a chord and an arc.

7) What are these 3D shapes called? a)   b)   c)

8) These two shapes are similar.
   What size is the unlabelled angle on the second shape?

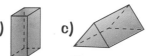

9) A plan of Alison's garden is shown on the right. Alison wants to
   put a fence around the perimeter of her garden, leaving only the gap
   that is shown. How many metres of fencing should Alison buy?

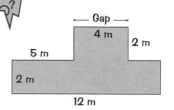

10) Clive is re-carpeting his lounge, which is rectangular. The room is 12 m long and 7 m wide.
    The carpet he wants costs £12 per m². How much will it cost Clive to carpet his lounge?

11) Jane has been asked to design packaging to hold 30 cm³ of washing powder.
    The packaging must be a prism.
    Sketch a possible design for the box and state its dimensions.

12) 1 mile = 1.6 km. How many miles is 27 km? Give it to the nearest mile.

13) 1 kg = 2.2 lbs. Kevin is filling in a form to join the gym and needs to give his weight in kg.
    He knows he weighs 10 st 4 lbs. How much is this in kg? (1 stone = 14 pounds.)

14) Laura is planning a walk in the countryside. The route she has planned is 15 km long.
    Laura knows that she walks at an average speed of 4 km/h. It gets dark at 5 pm.
    What is the latest time Laura should set off walking in order to get back before dark?

More Percentages

In an exam you might be asked to <u>compare</u> two numbers using <u>percentages</u>. Wowsers.
And by some happy coincidence that's what this page is all about.

Comparing Numbers using Percentages

This is a common type of percentage question.

> ### Give 'one number' AS A PERCENTAGE OF 'another number'

For example, "Express £2 <u>as a percentage of</u> £20." This is the method to use:

The FDP Method:

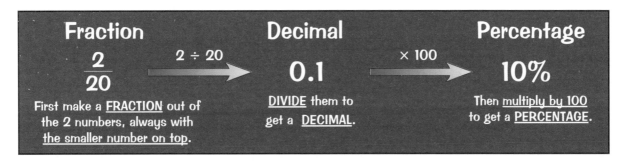

Fraction
$$\frac{2}{20}$$
First make a <u>FRACTION</u> out of the 2 numbers, always with <u>the smaller number on top</u>.

$2 \div 20$ →

Decimal
0.1
<u>DIVIDE</u> them to get a <u>DECIMAL</u>.

$\times 100$ →

Percentage
10%
Then <u>multiply by 100</u> to get a <u>PERCENTAGE</u>.

Two Important Examples

1) "A shopkeeper buys pens at 8p each and sells them for 10p each.
    What is his profit <u>AS A PERCENTAGE</u>?"

<u>Answer</u>:   The two numbers we want to <u>compare</u> are the <u>PROFIT</u> (which is 2p)
    with the <u>ORIGINAL</u> cost (which is 8p). We then apply the FDP method:

> <u>Fraction</u> → <u>Decimal</u> → <u>Percentage</u>:
> $$\frac{2}{8} \rightarrow 0.25 \rightarrow \underline{25\%}$$

so the shopkeeper makes a <u>25% profit on the pens</u>.

2) "In a sale, a tennis racket is reduced in price from £60 to £48.
    What <u>PERCENTAGE REDUCTION</u> is this?"

<u>Answer</u>:   The two numbers we want to <u>compare</u> are the <u>REDUCTION</u> (which is £12
    and the <u>ORIGINAL VALUE</u> (which is £60). We then apply the FDP method:

> <u>Fraction</u> → <u>Decimal</u> → <u>Percentage</u>:
> $$\frac{12}{60} \rightarrow 0.2 \rightarrow \underline{20\%}$$

63% of all statistics are made up...

So, the 'ole FDP method comes in handy here too. Time to check what you've learnt from this page...

1) A house increases in value from £140 000 to £182 000.
    What is the increase in value of the house as a percentage?

Percentages and Reciprocals

Important Example — adding VAT

E.g. A plumber's bill for fixing a small leak is £98 + VAT.
The VAT is charged at 17.5%. **WORK OUT THE TOTAL BILL.**

<u>Answer:</u> First find 17.5% of £98 using the standard method:

1) 17.5% of £98

2) $\frac{17.5}{100} \times 98$

3) 17.5 ÷ 100 × 98 = 17.15 = <u>£17.15</u>

This £17.15 is the VAT which then <u>has to be ADDED</u> to the £98 to give the <u>FINAL BILL</u>:
£98 + £17.15 = <u>£115.15</u>

Reciprocals — Learn these 4 Facts

1) The reciprocal of a number is '<u>one over</u>' the number. ⟹ The reciprocal of 5 = $\frac{1}{5}$.

2) You can find the reciprocal of a fraction by turning it <u>upside down</u>. ⟹ The reciprocal of $\frac{3}{8} = \frac{8}{3}$.

3) A number <u>multiplied by its reciprocal</u> gives <u>1</u>. ⟹ $\frac{6}{7} \times \frac{7}{6} = 1$

4) 0 has no reciprocal because <u>you can't divide anything by 0</u>.

The ⅟ₓ (or x⁻¹) Button Makes Reciprocals much Easier

This has two very useful functions:

1) <u>Making divisions a bit slicker</u> E.g. if you already have 2.3456326 in the display and
you want to do 12 ÷ 2.3456326, then you can just press ÷ 12 = ⅟ₓ = , which does
the division <u>the wrong way up</u> and then <u>flips it the right way up</u>.

2) <u>Analysing decimals</u> to see if they might be rational,
e.g. if the display is 0.142857142 and you press ⅟ₓ = you'll get 7, meaning it was $\frac{1}{7}$ before.

Never trust reciprocals — they're always trying to get one over on you...

Learn all the <u>bits and bobs</u> on this page then <u>turn over</u> and see how much you can remember. Try this:
1) A garage charges £60 + VAT for a car repair.
What is the total cost of the repair?

Solving Equations

The 'proper' way to <u>solve equations</u> is shown on the next page. In practice the 'proper' way can be pretty difficult so there's a lot to be said for the much easier methods shown below.

The drawback with these is that you can't always use them on very complicated equations. In most Exam questions though, they do just fine.

1) The 'Common Sense' Approach

The trick here is to realise that the unknown quantity 'x' is after all just a number and the 'equation' is just a cryptic clue to help you find it.

Example: "Solve this equation: $3x + 4 = 46$"
(i.e. find what number x is)

<u>Answer:</u> This is what you should say to yourself:

> "<u>Something + 4 = 46</u>" hmm, so that 'something' must be 42.
>
> So that means $3x = 42$, which means '3 times something = 42'
>
> So it must be $42 \div 3$ which is 14 so <u>x = 14</u>

In other words don't think of it as algebra, but as '<u>Find the mystery number</u>'.

2) The Trial and Error Method

This is a perfectly good method, and although it won't work every time, it usually does, especially if the answer is a <u>whole number</u>.

The <u>big secret of trial and error</u> methods is to find <u>TWO OPPOSITE CASES</u> and keep taking values <u>IN BETWEEN</u> them.

In other words, find a number that makes the <u>Right Hand Side bigger</u>, and then one that makes the <u>Left Hand Side bigger</u>, and then try values <u>in between them</u>.

Example: "Solve for x: $3x + 5 = 21 - 5x$"
(i.e. find the number x)

<u>Answer:</u>

> Try x=1: $3 + 5 = 21 - 5$, $8 = 16$ — no good, <u>RHS too big</u>
>
> Try x=3: $9 + 5 = 21 - 15$, $14 = 6$ — no good, <u>now LHS too big</u>

SO TRY IN BETWEEN: x = 2: $6 + 5 = 21 - 10$, $11 = 11$, YES, so <u>x = 2</u>.

But I'm innocent your honour — this trial is an error...

~~Loan those two methods.~~ No. ~~Learn these to meatheads.~~ No. <u>Learn these two methods</u>. Splendid.

1) Solve: $4x - 12 = 20$
2) Solve: $3x + 5 = 5x - 9$

Solving Equations

The 'proper' way of solving equations isn't tooooo difficult... it just needs lots of practice.

3) The 'Proper' Way

> **Golden Rules**
> 1) Always do the SAME thing to both sides of the equation.
> 2) To get rid of something, do the opposite.
>   The opposite of + is – and the opposite of – is +.
>   The opposite of × is ÷ and the opposite of ÷ is ×.
> 3) Keep going until you have a letter on its own.

Example 1: Solve $5x = 15$

$$5x = 15$$
$$\underline{x = 3}$$

5x means $5 \times x$, so do the opposite — divide both sides by 5.

Example 2: Solve $\frac{p}{3} = 2$

$$\frac{p}{3} = 2$$
$$\underline{p = 6}$$

$\frac{p}{3}$ means $p \div 3$, so do the opposite — multiply both sides by 3.

Example 3: Solve $4y - 3 = 17$

$$4y - 3 = 17$$
$$4y = 20$$
$$\underline{y = 5}$$

The opposite of –3 is +3 so add 3 to both sides.

The opposite of ×4 is ÷4 so divide both sides by 4.

Example 4: Solve $2(x + 3) = 11$

$$2(x + 3) = 11$$
$$x + 3 = 5.5$$
$$\underline{x = 2.5}$$

The opposite of ×2 is ÷2 so divide both sides by 2.

The opposite of +3 is –3 so subtract 3 from both sides.

Example 5: Solve $3x + 5 = 5x + 7$

there are x's on both sides, so subtract 3x from both sides. 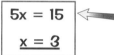 $3x + 5 = 5x + 7$

the opposite of +7 is –7, so subtract 7 from each side. $5 = 2x + 7$

the opposite of ×2 is ÷2, so divide each side by 2. $-2 = 2x$

$$\underline{-1 = x}$$

4) Rearranging Formulas

You do this in exactly the same way that you solve equations — watch...

Example 6: Rearrange the formula $q = 3p + 4$ to make p the subject:

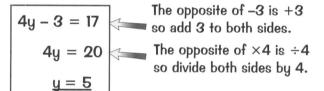

The opposite of +4 is –4 so take 4 from both sides.

The opposite of ×3 is ÷3 so divide both sides by 3.

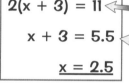

$$q = 3p + 4$$
$$q - 4 = 3p$$
$$\frac{q - 4}{3} = p$$

Dear Jim — could you fix it for me to make P the subject of this formula...

It's always good to know the proper way to solve equations, just in case you get thrown a curveball in the exam and they give you a real nightmare of an equation to solve.

1) Solve these equations: a) $3x + 1 = 13$ b) $\frac{q}{4} = 8$ c) $5y + 4 = 2y - 2$
2) Rearrange this formula to make b the subject: $2(b - 3) = a$

Trial and Improvement

This is a good method for finding approximate answers to equations that don't have simple whole number answers. Although it basically boils down to trial and error, there is a <u>clear method</u> which you must <u>learn</u> if you want to get it right...

Method

1) <u>SUBSTITUTE TWO INITIAL VALUES</u> into the equation that give <u>OPPOSITE CASES</u>.

Opposite cases means <u>one answer too big, one too small</u>. If they don't give opposite cases <u>try again</u>.

2) Choose your next value <u>IN BETWEEN</u> the previous two, and <u>PUT IT</u> into the equation.

<u>Continue the process</u>, choosing new values <u>between the two closest opposite cases</u>, (and preferably nearer to the one which is closer to the answer you want).

3) After only 3 or 4 steps you should have <u>2 NUMBERS</u> which are to the right degree of accuracy but <u>DIFFER BY 1 IN THE LAST DIGIT</u>.

E.g. if you had to get your answer to 2 DP, you'd eventually end up with say <u>5.43</u> and <u>5.44</u>, with these giving <u>OPPOSITE</u> cases.

4) Now take the <u>EXACT MIDDLE VALUE</u> to decide which is the answer you want.

E.g. for 5.43 and 5.44, you'd try 5.435 to see if the real answer was <u>between 5.43 and 5.435</u> or between <u>5.435 and 5.44</u>.

Example

"The equation $x^3 + x = 40$ has a solution between 3 and 3.5. Find this solution to 1 DP"

> Try x = 3 $3^3 + 3 = 30$ (Too small)
> Try x = 3.5 $3.5^3 + 3.5 = 46.375$ (Too big)

← (2 opposite cases)

40 is what we want and it's closer to 46.375 than it is to 30 so we'll choose our next value for x closer to 3.5 than 3.

> Try x = 3.3 $3.3^3 + 3.3 = 39.237$ (Too small)

Good, this is very close, but we need to see if 3.4 is still too big or too small:

> Try x = 3.4 $3.4^0 + 3.4 = 42.704$ (Too big)

Good, now we know that <u>the answer must be between 3.3 and 3.4</u>.
To find out which one it's nearest to, we have to try the <u>EXACT MIDDLE VALUE</u>:   3.35

> Try x = 3.35 $3.35^3 + 3.35 = 40.945$ (Too big)

This tells us with certainty that the solution must be between 3.3 (too small) and 3.35 (too big), and so to 1 DP <u>it must round down to 3.3</u>. ANSWER = 3.3

If at first you don't succeed — improve and trial again...

To get this method nailed, you must <u>learn the 4 steps above</u>. Do it now, and practise until you can <u>write them down without having to look back at them</u>. I said now. I can still see you — do it now!
The equation $x^3 - 2x = 1$ has a solution between 1 and 2. Find it to 1 DP.

Inequalities

I'm not going to lie to you, some of this is a bit nasty. But I reckon you're up to it...

The 4 Inequality Symbols:

> means 'Greater than'   ≥ means 'Greater than or equal to'
< means 'Less than'   ≤ means 'Less than or equal to'

REMEMBER, the one at the BIG end is BIGGEST

so 'x > 4' and '4 < x' BOTH say: 'x is greater than 4'

I > All of you.

Algebra With Inequalities — this is generally a bit tricky

The thing to remember here is that inequalities are just like regular equations in the sense that all the normal rules of algebra apply WITH ONE BIG EXCEPTION:

$5x < x + 2$
$5x = x + 2$

Whenever you MULTIPLY OR DIVIDE BY A NEGATIVE NUMBER, you must FLIP THE INEQUALITY SIGN.

You Can Show Inequalities on Number Lines

This number line shows the solution $-5 \leq x \leq 5$:

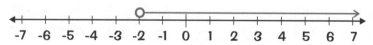

You need to use filled circles (●) to show that the solution includes the numbers 5 and -5.

If your inequality had a < or > instead of a ≤ or ≥, you'd draw an open circle (O).

Example   "Solve 5x < 6x +2. Show your answer on the number line below."

Subtract 6x from both sides: $5x - 6x < 2$

combining the x-terms gives: $-x < 2$

To get rid of the '–' in front of x you need to divide both sides by -1 — but remember that means the '<' has to be flipped as well, which gives:

$x > -2$ i.e. 'x is greater than -2' is the answer

(The < has flipped around into a >, because we divided by a –ve number)

This answer, $x > -2$, can be displayed on a number line like this:

```
  <--+--+--+--+--+--○--+--+--+--+--+--+--+--+-->
     -7 -6 -5 -4 -3 -2 -1  0  1  2  3  4  5  6  7
```

Algebra with inequalities? Go and wash your mouth out young man...

Yikes, I'm glad that's over. Right, learn: The 4 Inequality Signs, the similarity with equations and the One Big Exception. And then have a crack at these beautiful questions:

1) Solve this inequality: $4x + 3 \leq 6x + 7$.

2) Solve the inequalities and find the integer values of x which satisfy both:
    $2x + 9 \geq 1$ and $4x < 6 + x$

Quadratic Graphs

Equations with an x^2 term in them are called quadratic equations. The graphs of these equations always have the same SYMMETRICAL bucket shape.

If the x^2 bit is positive (i.e. $+x^2$) the bucket is the normal way up, but if the x^2 bit has a "minus" in front of it (i.e. $-x^2$) then the bucket is upside down. The graphs get steeper and steeper but never vertical — remember this when you're drawing them.

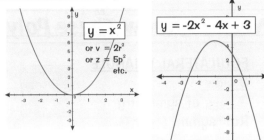

Most questions follow a set pattern...

Fill in the Table of Values

Example: "Fill in the table of values for the equation $y = x^2 + 2x - 3$ and draw the graph."

x	-5	-4	-3	-2	-1	0	1	2	3
y		5		-3	-4	-3	0		

Work out each point very carefully, writing down all your working. To check you're doing it right, make sure you can reproduce the y-values they've already given you.

E.g. If $x = 1$, $y = (1)^2 + (2 \times 1) - 3 = 1 + 2 - 3 = 0$.

Draw the Curve

1) **PLOT THE POINTS CAREFULLY,** and don't mix up the x and y values.

2) The points should form a **COMPLETELY SMOOTH CURVE.** If they don't, they're wrong.

   NEVER EVER let one point drag your line off in some ridiculous direction. When a graph is generated from an equation, you never get spikes or lumps — only MISTAKES.

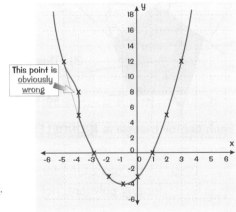

This point is obviously wrong

Use the Graph to Answer a Question

Example: "Use your graph to solve the equation $x^2 + 2x - 3 = 0$."

1) Look — the equation you've been asked to solve is what you get when you put $y=0$ into the graph's equation, $y = x^2 + 2x - 3$.

2) To solve the equation, all you do is read the x-values where $y = 0$, i.e. where it crosses the x-axis.

3) So the solutions are $x = -3$ and $x = +1$. (Quadratic eqns usually have 2 solutions.)

Make sure your graphs are smoother than a polished kipper...

Learn the details of the method above for drawing quadratic graphs and solving the equation.

Plot the graph of $y = x^2 - x - 6$ (use x-values from -4 to 5).

Use your graph to solve the equation $x^2 - x - 6 = 0$.

Regular Polygons

A <u>polygon</u> is a <u>many-sided shape</u>. A <u>regular</u> polygon is one where all the <u>sides</u> and <u>angles</u> are the same. The regular polygons are a never-ending series of shapes with some fancy features.

You Need to Know These Polygons

EQUILATERAL TRIANGLE
<u>3 sides</u>
<u>3 lines</u> of symmetry
Rot^{nl} symm. <u>order 3</u>

SQUARE
<u>4 sides</u>
<u>4 lines</u> of symmetry
Rot^{nl} symm. <u>order 4</u>

REGULAR PENTAGON
<u>5 sides</u>
<u>5 lines</u> of symmetry
Rot^{nl} symm. <u>order 5</u>

REGULAR HEXAGON
<u>6 sides</u>
<u>6 lines</u> of symmetry
Rot^{nl} symm. <u>order 6</u>

REGULAR HEPTAGON
<u>7 sides</u>
<u>7 lines</u> of symmetry
Rot^{nl} symm. <u>order 7</u>
(A 50p piece is like a heptagon)

REGULAR OCTAGON
<u>8 sides</u>
<u>8 lines</u> of symmetry
Rot^{nl} symm. <u>order 8</u>

You also need to know the <u>next two</u>, but I'm not drawing them for you. <u>Learn their names</u>:

REGULAR NONAGON
<u>9 sides</u>, etc. etc.

REGULAR DECAGON
<u>10 sides</u>, etc. etc.

Polygons Have Interior and Exterior Angles

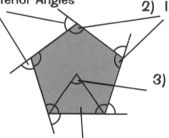

1) Exterior Angles

2) Interior Angles

3) This angle is always the same as the Exterior Angles.

4) Each sector triangle is <u>ISOSCELES</u>.

There are 4 formulas to learn:

$$\text{EXTERIOR ANGLE} = \frac{360°}{n}$$

$$\text{INTERIOR ANGLE} = 180° - \text{EXTERIOR ANGLE}$$

$$\text{SUM OF EXTERIOR ANGLES} = 360°$$

$$\text{SUM OF INTERIOR ANGLES} = (n-2) \times 180°$$

Note — the two SUM formulas above work for <u>any</u> polygons, not just regular ones.

(n is the number of sides)

Regular Polygons have Loads of Symmetry

1) The pentagon shown here has <u>only 3 different angles</u> in the whole diagram.

2) This is <u>typical of regular polygons</u>. They display an amazing amount of symmetry.

3) With a regular polygon, if two angles <u>look</u> the same, they <u>will be</u>. That's not a rule you should normally apply in geometry, and anyway you'll need to <u>prove</u> they're equal.

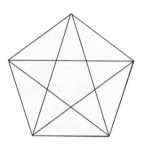

EXCLUSIVE: Heptagon lottery winner says "I'm still just a regular guy"...

Lots to learn on this page. But as long as you're familiar with the word regular, you're half way there.

1) What is a regular polygon?
2) Name the first six of them.
3) Work out the two key angles for a regular pentagon
4) And for a 12-sided regular polygon.
5) Draw a regular <u>pentagon</u> and a regular <u>hexagon</u> and put in all their lines of symmetry.

Congruence and Tessellation

Shapes can be <u>congruent</u>. And I bet you really want to know what that means —
I can already picture your eager face. Well, lucky you — I've written a page all about it.

Congruent — Same Shape, Same Size

<u>Congruence</u> is another ridiculous maths word which sounds really complicated but it's not:

> If two shapes are **CONGRUENT**, they are simply **THE SAME**
> — the **SAME SIZE** and the **SAME SHAPE**.

That's all it is. Just make sure you know the word.

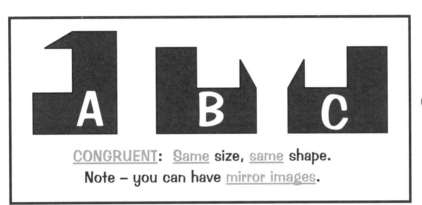

<u>CONGRUENT</u>: <u>Same</u> size, <u>same</u> shape.
Note — you can have <u>mirror images</u>.

There ain't room for the two of us in this town, pal.

Tessellations — 'Tiling patterns with no gaps'

You must have done loads of these, but don't forget what
the name '<u>tessellation</u>' means — '<u>a tiling pattern with no gaps</u>':

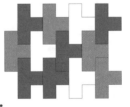

In the exam you can be asked to tessellate regular or irregular polygons.
Still, at least drawing a pretty pattern is a fun way to pick up marks.

EXAMPLE: Baz has bought two types
of tile to cover his kitchen floor.
On the grid, show how the tiles will tessellate.

Remember — your pattern shouldn't have any g aps.

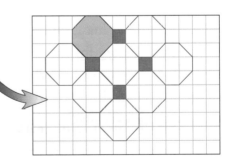

Pizza and a frisbee — same shape and size but don't get them confused...

Know what congruence and tessellation mean inside-out.

1) Which of these shapes are congruent?

i) ii) iii)  iv)

Pythagoras' Theorem

Once upon a time there lived a clever chap called Pythagoras. He came up with a clever theorem...

Pythagoras' Theorem is Used on Right Angled Triangles

PYTHAGORAS' THEOREM is a handy little formula for RIGHT-ANGLED TRIANGLES.
What it does is let you find the length of the third side when you know two of them.

The formula for Pythagoras' theorem is: $a^2 + b^2 = h^2$ where a and b are

the short sides and h is the long side of the triangle (called the hypotenuse)
Remember that Pythagoras can only be used on RIGHT-ANGLED TRIANGLES.

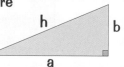

The trouble is, the formula can be quite difficult to use. Instead, it's a lot better
to just remember these three simple steps, which work every time:

1) Square Them   SQUARE THE TWO NUMBERS that you are given,
(use the x^2 button if you've got your calculator.)

2) Add or Subtract   To find the longest side, ADD the two squared numbers.
To find a shorter side, SUBTRACT the smaller one from the larger.

3) Square Root   Once you've got your answer, take the SQUARE ROOT
(use the √ button on your calculator).

EXAMPLE 1: "Find the missing side in the triangle shown."

1) Square them: $5^2 = 25$, $3^2 = 9$

2) You want to find a shorter side, so SUBTRACT: $25 - 9 = 16$

3) Square root: $\sqrt{16} = 4$
   So the missing side $= 4\,m$

(You should always ask yourself: "Is it a sensible answer?" — in this case you can say "YES,
because it's shorter than 5 m, as it should be since 5 m is the longest side, but not too much shorter")

EXAMPLE 2: "Find the length of the line segment shown."

1) Work out how far across and up it is from A to B

2) Treat this exactly like a normal triangle...

3) Square them: $3^2 = 9$, $4^2 = 16$

4) You want to find the longest side (the hypotenuse),
   so ADD: $9 + 16 = 25$

5) Square root: $\sqrt{25} = 5$
   So the length of the line segment = 5 units

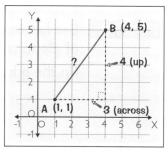

Ah, the mighty right-angled triangle never ceases to amaze...

... well, maybe not. But it's still pretty clever stuff. Learn this page then have a go at these beauties:

1) Apply the above method to find the missing side BC:

2) Another triangle has sides of 5 m, 12 m and 13 m.
   Is it a right-angled triangle? How do you know?

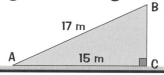

Solids and Nets

You might think you know some of this already, but I bet you don't know it all. There's only one thing for it...

Surface Area and Nets

1) **A NET** is just **A SOLID SHAPE FOLDED OUT FLAT**.
2) The surface area of a solid is just the area of all of the shape's faces added together.
3) So obviously: **SURFACE AREA OF SOLID = AREA OF NET**.

There are 4 nets that you need to know really well for the Exam, and they're shown below. They may well ask you to draw one of these nets and then work out its area.

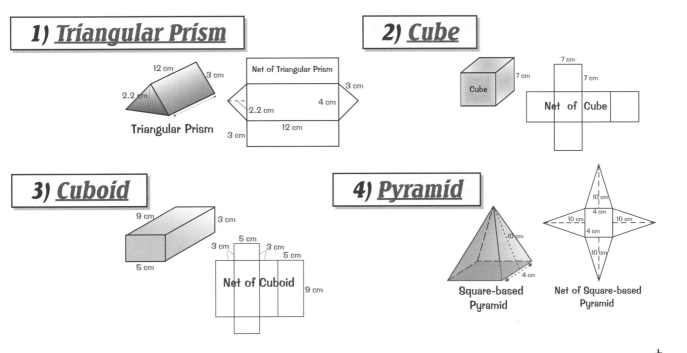

1) Triangular Prism

2) Cube

3) Cuboid

4) Pyramid

Projections Show Different Viewpoints

A 'projection' shows the shape of an object from either the front, side or back — they're usually known as 'elevations'. A 'plan' shows the view from above. Projections and plans are always drawn to scale.

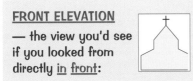

FRONT ELEVATION
— the view you'd see if you looked from directly in front:

SIDE ELEVATION
— the view you'd see if you looked from directly to one side:

PLAN
— the view you'd see if you looked from directly above:

If they're feeling really mean (and they often are), you might get asked to draw a 3D shape from elevation and plan drawings.

What's the area of Annette — bit of a personal question...

Righty-ho, time to learn all about nets, surface area and the types of projection. Such fun.
Cover up the page, then scribble the net for a triangular prism, a cube, a cuboid and a pyramid.
1) Draw a plan, front and side elevations of your own house.

The Four Transformations

Objects can be transformed by changing their <u>position</u> or <u>size</u>, <u>spinning</u> or <u>reflecting</u> them.

Four Types of Transformation

Translation— ONE Detail
Enlargement — TWO Details
Rotation— THREE Details
Reflection — ONE Detail
Y (The Y doesn't stand for anything)

1) Use the word TERRY to remember the 4 types.
2) You must always give <u>all the details</u> for each type.

1) Translation

A translation is just a <u>SLIDE</u>. You must specify <u>how far along</u> and <u>how far up</u> the translation is.

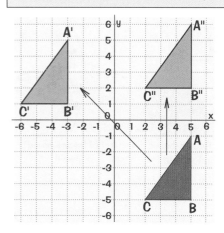

ABC to A'B'C' is a <u>translation</u> of <u>8 left and 6 up</u>.
ABC to A''B''C'' is a <u>translation</u> of <u>7 up</u>.

You can describe translations with <u>vectors</u> which look like this. x is the number of spaces <u>right</u>, y is the number of spaces <u>up</u>. $\begin{pmatrix} \xrightarrow{x} \\ \uparrow y \end{pmatrix}$

As vectors, the translations shown in the diagram are: $\begin{pmatrix} -8 \\ 6 \end{pmatrix}$ and $\begin{pmatrix} 0 \\ 7 \end{pmatrix}$

2) Enlargement

You must give these <u>2 details</u>: 1) The <u>SCALE FACTOR</u>
2) The <u>CENTRE</u> of Enlargement

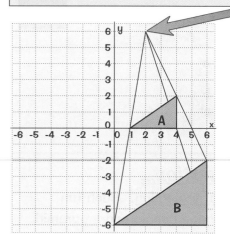

From <u>A to B</u> is an enlargement of <u>scale factor 2</u>, and <u>centre (2,6)</u>.

<u>N.B.</u> Lengths <u>doubled</u>, distances from centre <u>doubled too</u>.

With enlargement, the ANGLES of the object remain <u>unchanged</u>. The RATIOS of the lengths of the sides, and the object's ORIENTATION remain <u>unchanged</u>. The size and position <u>do</u> change.

The Four Transformations

Two down, two to go...

3) Rotation

You must give these <u>3 details</u>:
1) <u>ANGLE</u> turned
2) <u>DIRECTION</u> (Clockwise or Anti-clockwise)
3) <u>CENTRE</u> of Rotation

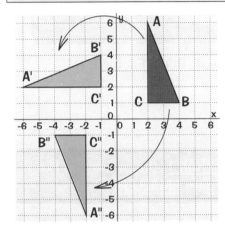

ABC to A'B'C' is a Rotation of <u>90°</u>, <u>anticlockwise</u>, <u>ABOUT</u> the origin.

ABC to A''B''C'' is a Rotation of <u>half a turn (180°)</u>, <u>clockwise</u>, <u>ABOUT the origin</u>.

(For half-turns, it doesn't actually matter if you go clockwise or anticlockwise.)

The only things that change in a rotation are the **POSITION** and the **ORIENTATION** of the object. <u>Everything else</u> remains <u>unchanged</u>.

4) Reflection

You must give this <u>ONE detail</u>: The <u>MIRROR LINE</u>

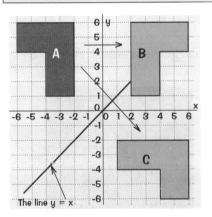

A to B is a <u>reflection IN the y-axis</u>.

A to C is a <u>reflection IN the line y=x</u>.

With reflection, the **POSITION** and **ORIENTATION** of the object are the <u>only things that change</u>.

The line y = x

<u>Wish someone would translate these pages for me...</u>

Another two pages down. Hurrah. Before you move on you need to:
<u>LEARN the names</u> of the <u>Four Transformations</u> and the details for each.
Then, when you think you know it, <u>turn over and write it all down</u>.
Finally, do a dance to celebrate. Any dance will do.

1) Describe <u>fully</u> these 4 transformations:

   A→B,   B→C,   C→A,   A→D

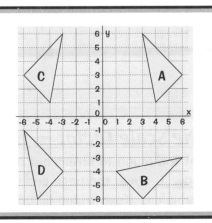

Enlargements

Enlargements are a really important type of transformation — so much so that here's an extra two pages on them, created especially for you. I know, I know, I'm too kind...

Scale Factors

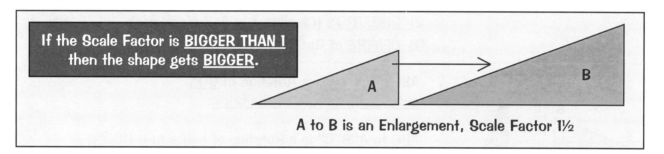

If the Scale Factor is **BIGGER THAN 1** then the shape gets **BIGGER**.

A to B is an Enlargement, Scale Factor 1½

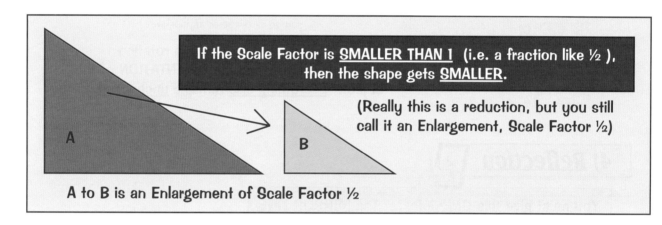

If the Scale Factor is **SMALLER THAN 1** (i.e. a fraction like ½), then the shape gets **SMALLER**.

(Really this is a reduction, but you still call it an Enlargement, Scale Factor ½)

A to B is an Enlargement of Scale Factor ½

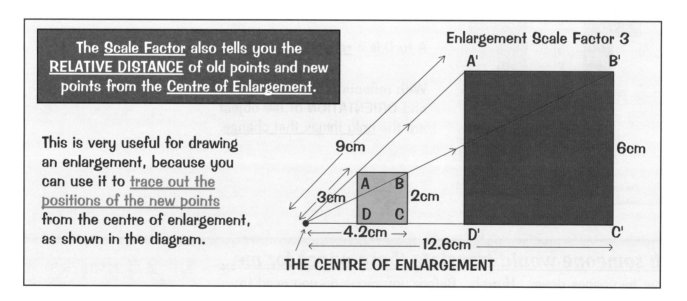

The Scale Factor also tells you the **RELATIVE DISTANCE** of old points and new points from the Centre of Enlargement.

This is very useful for drawing an enlargement, because you can use it to trace out the positions of the new points from the centre of enlargement, as shown in the diagram.

Enlargement Scale Factor 3

9cm
6cm
3cm
2cm
4.2cm
12.6cm
THE CENTRE OF ENLARGEMENT

The Scale Factor — it's time... to face... the diet...

Not too much to stress out over here — **LEARN everything on the page**, then **when you think you know it**, cover the page and **write it all down** from **memory**. Make sure you include the sketches and examples. Keep trying till you can. What a fun game that'll be. I'm almost jealous. Almost...

Enlargements

More on enlargements...

Use the Formula Triangle for Calculations

The lengths of the big and small shapes are related to the Scale Factor by this very important <u>Formula Triangle</u> which you must learn:

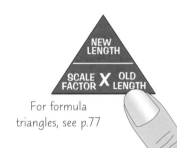

For formula triangles, see p.77

EXAMPLE: Find the missing width, x, in the diagram.

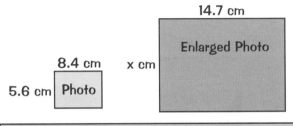

14.7 cm

Enlarged Photo

8.4 cm

x cm

5.6 cm Photo

To find the width of the enlarged photo we <u>use the formula triangle TWICE</u>, (firstly to find the <u>Scale Factor</u>, and then to find the <u>missing side</u>):

1) <u>Scale Factor</u> = New length ÷ Old length = 14.7 ÷ 8.4 = <u>1.75</u>
2) <u>New width</u> = Scale Factor × Old width = 1.75 × 5.6 = <u>9.8 cm</u>

But without the formula triangle you're scuppered (Just like this fish)

Note — you can use the formula triangle to find <u>perimeters</u> in exactly the same way as lengths. E.g. a square with sides 1 cm is enlarged by a scale factor of 2. New perimeter = scale factor × old perimeter = 2 × 4 = 8 cm.

Areas and Volumes of Enlargements

Ho ho! This little joker catches everybody out. The increase in area and volume is **BIGGER** than the scale factor. <u>For example</u>, if the Scale Factor is 2, the lengths are <u>twice as big</u>, each area is <u>4 times</u> as big, and the volume is <u>8 times</u> as big. The rule is this:

For a Scale Factor n:

The <u>SIDES</u> are	n times bigger	
The <u>AREAS</u> are	n^2 times bigger	
The <u>VOLUMES</u> are	n^3 times bigger	Simple... but <u>VERY FORGETTABLE</u>

EXAMPLE: Two bottles of water are similar. They have heights of 20 cm and 30 cm. If the volume of the smaller bottle is 2 litres, find the volume of the larger bottle.

1) <u>Scale Factor n</u> = New height ÷ Old height = 30 ÷ 20 = <u>1.5</u>
2) <u>New volume</u> = Old volume × (Scale Factor)³ = 2 × 1.5³ = <u>6.75 litres</u>

"Twice as much learning, 4 times better results, 8 times more fun...

...with a scale factor of 2, CGP's the guide for you". It's our new slogan. Pretty good isn't it...

1) Two triangles which are similar have heights of 5 cm and 45 cm respectively. The smaller triangle has an area of 30 cm². Find the area of the larger triangle.
2) Two similar cones have base diameters of 20 cm and 50 cm. If the volume of the smaller one is 120 cm³, find the volume of the other one.

Combinations of Transformations

In the Exam they might be <u>horrid</u> to you and <u>stick two transformations together</u>, and then ask you what combination gets you from shape A to shape B. Be <u>ready</u>. Be <u>prepared</u>. Don't let them <u>win</u>.

The Better You Know Them All — The Easier it is

These kinds of question aren't so bad — but <u>ONLY</u> if you've <u>LEARNT</u> the <u>four transformations</u> on pages 90-92 <u>really well</u> — if you don't know them, then you certainly won't do too well at spotting a <u>combination</u> of one followed by another. That's because the method is basically '<u>Try it and see...</u>'

Example:

"What combination of two transformations takes you from triangle A to triangle B?"

(There's usually a few different ways of getting from one shape to the other — but remember you only need to find <u>ONE</u> of them.)

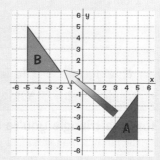

METHOD: Try an obvious transformation first, and see...

If you <u>think</u> about it, the answer can <u>only</u> be a combination of two of the <u>four types</u> shown on pages 90 and 91, so you can immediately start to <u>narrow it down</u>:

1) Since the shapes are the <u>same size</u> we can <u>rule out enlargements</u>.

2) Next, <u>try a reflection</u> (in either the x-axis or the y-axis). Here we've tried a reflection in the <u>y-axis</u>, to give shape A':

3) You should now easily be able to see the <u>final step</u> from A' to B — it's a <u>translation</u> of $\begin{pmatrix} 0 \\ 6 \end{pmatrix}$

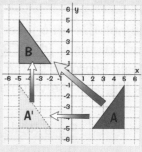

And that's it <u>DONE</u> — from A to B is simply a combination of:

A <u>reflection in the y-axis</u> followed by a <u>translation of</u> $\begin{pmatrix} 0 \\ 6 \end{pmatrix}$

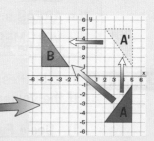

At least that's <u>one answer</u> anyway. If instead we decided to reflect it in the <u>x-axis</u> first (as shown here) then we'd get another answer (see questions below) — but both are right.

Not bothered about shapes — how do I get from one topic to another...

Seriously, enough with all the transformations. We'll make this the last page.

1) What pair of transformations will convert shape C into shape D? What pair will convert shape D to shape C?

2) In the example above, find the other transformation needed to get to shape B after reflecting shape A in the x-axis.

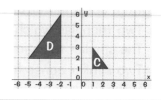

Revision Summary for Unit 3 — Part 1

WHAT YOU'RE SUPPOSED TO DO HERE is.... well you probably know by now.

Go on, use your Unit 3 know-how and give these questions a go.

1) It cost Asik £150 to print 300 programmes for the school play.
How much should he sell each programme for in order to get his money back?

2) A DVD player costs £50 plus VAT. If VAT is 17.5%, how much does the DVD player cost?

3) Carl has £35 to spend. He wants to use a 20%-off voucher
to buy a top that should cost £45. Can he afford the top?

4) What's the reciprocal of a) 6   b) 12   c) ½?

5) Solve these equations:
a) $2x + 3 = 7$ b) $33 - 4x = 7x$ c) $5(x + 5) = -10$

6) For each of these, make y the subject:
a) $6 - y = x$ b) $11 + 2y = x$ c) $y/3 = 7x + 3$

7) If $x^2 = 30$, find x accurate to one decimal place. (Trial and Improvement)

8) Solve these inequalities:
a) $5x < 25$ b) $20 - 5x > 25$ c) $-6x < 30$ d) $10x > 170 - 7x$

9) Say if each of the following are straight-line equations or quadratics.
a) $x + 3 = y$ b) $y + x^2 = 2$ c) $y/2 = 1 - 2x$ d) $y^2 = x$

10) Work out the exterior and interior angles for a regular octagon (8 sides).

11) What is congruence? On a grid, draw a tessellating pattern of parallelograms.

12) A museum has a flight of stairs up to its front door (see diagram).
A ramp is to be put over the top of the stairs for wheelchair users.
Calculate the length that the ramp would need to be.

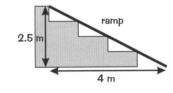

13) An architect is planning an extension
to a house, shown on the right.
Using the scale 1 m : 1 cm, draw:
a) the side elevation   b) the front elevation
c) the plan view.

14) Do a sketch of these three solids and draw the net for each one:
a) A cube   b) A cuboid   c) A triangular prism

15) What transformation maps   a) shape A onto shape B?
b) shape C onto shape D?

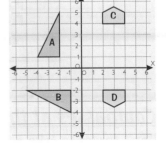

16) Julie wants a picture enlarging for a new frame.
Use the diagram to work out the
enlargement scale factor Julie needs.

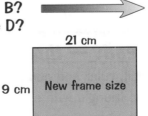

Unit 3 — Number, Algebra and Geometry 2

Triangle Construction

I just know that you're dying to draw some triangles about now. And that's so weird, because that's exactly what's coming up next in this uber-exciting quest to master GCSE maths. Spooky.

Follow the Steps to Construct a Triangle

'Construct' means <u>draw accurately</u> using <u>pencil</u>, <u>ruler</u> and <u>compasses</u>.

If you're told to <u>construct a triangle</u> and you're told <u>how long the three sides are</u>, this is what to do.

> 1) Draw a <u>**ROUGH SKETCH**</u> and <u>**LABEL THE LENGTHS**</u> of the sides.
> 2) Draw the <u>**BASE LINE**</u> using a ruler.
> 3) Draw <u>**TWO ARCS**</u>, one from <u>**EACH END**</u> of the base line, setting your compasses to the <u>**LENGTHS OF THE SIDES**</u>.
> 4) Draw lines from the <u>**ENDS OF THE BASE LINE**</u> to where the <u>**TWO ARCS CROSS**</u>.

Example: | Construct the triangle ABC where AB = 6 cm, BC = 4 cm, AC = 5 cm.

ANSWER:

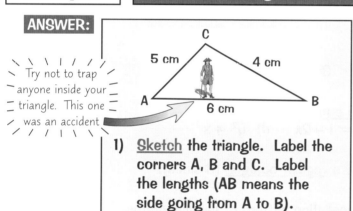

> Try not to trap anyone inside your triangle. This one was an accident

1) <u>Sketch</u> the triangle. Label the corners A, B and C. Label the lengths (AB means the side going from A to B).

2) Pick a side for the <u>base line</u> — it doesn't matter which one. We'll pick AB. Draw a line 6 cm long. Label the ends A and B.

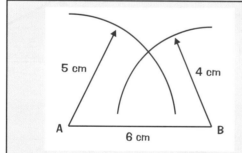

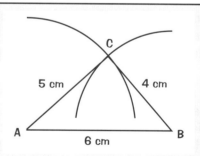

3) For AC, set the compasses to 5 cm, put the point at A and <u>draw an arc</u>. For BC, set the compasses to 4 cm, put the point at B and <u>draw an arc</u>.

4) Where the <u>arcs cross</u> is the point C. Draw a line from A to C and another line from B to C to finish your triangle.

Compasses at the ready — three, two, one... Construct...

Don't forget to take a pencil, ruler and compasses into the exam. Or you'll look like a plonker.
1) Construct an equilateral triangle with sides 5 cm.
2) Construct a triangle with sides 3 cm, 4 cm and 5 cm. Check it by measuring the sides.

Loci and Constructions

"Loci and constructions — what the monkey is that about" I hear you cry. Well, wonder no more...

Drawing Loci

A __LOCUS__ (another ridiculous maths word) is simply:

> __A LINE__ that shows __all the points which fit in with a given rule__

Make sure you __learn__ how to do these __PROPERLY__ using a __RULER AND COMPASSES__ as shown.

The locus of points which are 'A fixed distance from a given point'

This locus is simply a __CIRCLE__.

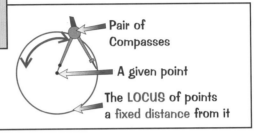

Pair of Compasses

A given point

The LOCUS of points a fixed distance from it

The locus of points which are 'A fixed distance from a given line'

This locus is an __OVAL SHAPE__.

It has __straight sides__ (drawn with a __ruler__) and __ends__ which are __perfect semicircles__ (drawn with __compasses__).

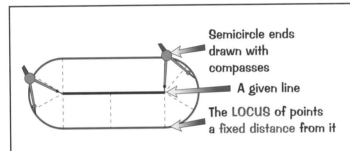

Semicircle ends drawn with compasses

A given line

The LOCUS of points a fixed distance from it

The locus of points which are 'Equidistant from two given lines'

1) Keep the compass setting __THE SAME__ while you make __all four marks__.

2) Make sure you __leave__ your compass marks __showing__.

3) You get __two equal angles__ — i.e. this __LOCUS__ is actually an __ANGLE BISECTOR__.

Equidistant just means 'the same distance'.

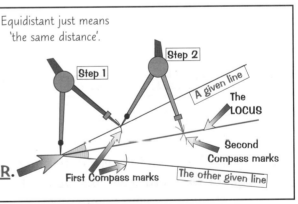

Step 1

Step 2

A given line

The LOCUS

Second Compass marks

First Compass marks

The other given line

The locus of points which are 'Equidistant from two given POINTS'

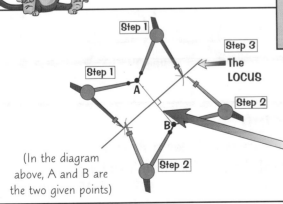

Step 1

Step 1

Step 3

The LOCUS

Step 2

Step 2

(In the diagram above, A and B are the two given points)

__This LOCUS__ is all the points which are the __same distance__ from A and B.

This time the locus is actually the __PERPENDICULAR BISECTOR__ of the line joining the two points.

Weird, scary, mutant monkey. Run... RUN...

Loci and Constructions

More on loci and constructions. Don't be alarmed by the floating, body-less hands. They're just there to point out the right diagram at the right time. Just pretend they're <u>regular</u> arrows.

Constructing accurate 60° angles

1) They may well ask you to draw an <u>accurate 60° angle</u>.

2) One place they're needed is for drawing an <u>equilateral triangle</u>.

3) Make sure you <u>follow the method</u> shown in this diagram, and that you can do it <u>entirely from memory</u>.

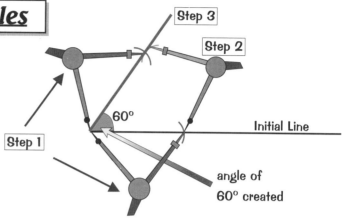

You can construct 30° angles and 45° angles by <u>bisecting</u> 60° and 90° angles.

Constructing accurate 90° angles

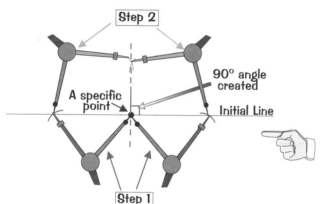

1) They might want you to draw an <u>accurate 90° angle</u>.

2) They won't accept it just done '<u>by eye</u>' or with a ruler — if you want to get the marks, you've got to do it <u>the proper way</u> with <u>compasses</u> like I've shown you here.

3) Make sure you can <u>follow the method</u> shown in this diagram.

Drawing the Perpendicular from a Point to a Line

1) This is similar to the one above but <u>not quite</u> the same — make sure you can do <u>both</u>.

2) Again, they won't accept it just done '<u>by eye</u>' or with a ruler — you've got to do it the <u>proper way</u> with <u>compasses</u>.

3) <u>Learn</u> the diagram.

If you need to draw a parallel line, just draw <u>a second line perpendicular to the first one you drew</u>.

Initial Line

Step 2 — This is the perpendicular required

90° angle created

Initial Line

The specific point

Step 1

If you're loci, you won't get tested on this stuff...

Haha — I crack myself up. But hilarious jokes aside, make sure you do learn these pages.
Start by covering them up and drawing an example of each of the four loci from memory.
Then draw an equilateral triangle and a square, both with fabulously accurate 60° and 90° angles.
Also, draw a line and a point and construct the perpendicular from the point to the line. Lovely.

Circles — Area and Circumference

Mmmm.... pi...

Area, Circumference and π

The CIRCUMFERENCE is the distance round the outside of the circle.
You should know the formulas for area and circumference...

<u>AREA</u> of <u>CIRCLE</u> = π × (radius)²   e.g. if the radius
is 4 cm, then
$$A = \pi \times r^2$$
A = 3.142×(4×4)
= <u>50 cm²</u> to the nearest cm²

<u>CIRCUMFERENCE</u> = π × Diameter
$$C = \pi \times D$$

π = 3.141592....
= <u>3.142</u> (approx)

The big thing to remember is that π (called "pi") is
just an <u>ordinary number</u> (3.14159...) which is usually
rounded off to 3.142. You can also use the π button
on your calculator (which is way more accurate).

And remember, it makes <u>no difference at all</u> whether the question gives you
the radius or the diameter, because whichever one they give you, it's <u>DEAD
EASY</u> to work out the other one — the diameter is always <u>DOUBLE</u> the radius.

Example 1:

"Find the circumference and the area of the circle shown below.
Give your answers to 1 decimal place."

<u>ANSWER:</u>
The radius = 5 cm, so the <u>diameter = 10 cm</u>   (easy huh?)

Formula for <u>circumference</u> is:
   C = π × D, so
   C = 3.142 × 10
     = <u>31.4 cm</u>

Formula for <u>AREA</u> is:
   A = π × r²
     = 3.142 × (5×5)
     = 3.142 × 25 = <u>78.6 cm²</u>

5 cm

Don't panic if you get
asked to find the areas
of semicircles or quarter
circles — just find
the area the full circle
would have, then halve
or quarter it. Easy.

Example 2:   The good old "Wagon Wheel" question:

This is a very common Exam question. "How many turns must a wheel of diameter
1.2 m make to go a distance of 12 m? Give your answer to 1 decimal place."

<u>ANSWER:</u>
Each full turn moves it <u>one full circumference</u> across the ground, so

1) find the circumference using "C = π × D" :   C = 3.142 × 1.2 = <u>3.7704 m</u>

2) then find how many times it fits into the distance travelled, by dividing:
    i.e.   12 m ÷ 3.7704 m = 3.2 to 1 d.p.   so the answer is <u>3.2 turns of the wheel</u>

History lesson — Wagon Wheels were a popular lunch box snack in 1993...

Make sure you understand both of these examples — ones just like them may well pop up in your exam.

1) A plate has a diameter of 14 cm. Find its area and circumference. Give your answers to the nearest
whole number, and remember to show all your working out.

2) How many complete turns will a hoop of diameter 2 m make if it rolls 240 m?

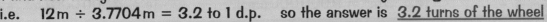

More Area and Volume

The cylinder, the tube, the Swiss roll...
However you think of it — you need to know how to find its <u>volume</u> and <u>surface area</u>.

Finding the Surface Area and Volume of a Cylinder

A cylinder is a bit like a prism (see p.75) so you
can use the same formulas as before — huzzah.

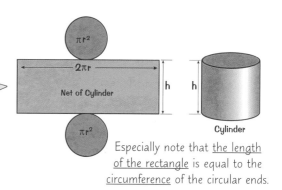

Net of Cylinder

Cylinder

Especially note that <u>the length
of the rectangle</u> is equal to the
<u>circumference</u> of the circular ends.

1) Surface Area

The net of a cylinder looks a bit like this
— the curved surface is just a rectangle.
So the total surface area of a cylinder will be the area of
this rectangle, plus the areas of the two circular ends.

> **Surface area of a CYLINDER = $2\pi rh + 2\pi r^2$**

2) Volume

Circular Prism
(or Cylinder)

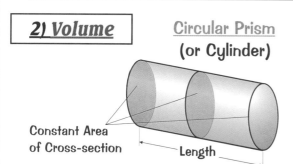

Constant Area
of Cross-section

Length

> **Volume of prism** = **Cross-sectional Area** × **length**

$$V = \pi r^2 \times l$$

Converting Area and Volume Measurements

> $1\,m^2 = 100\,cm \times 100\,cm = 10\,000\,cm^2$

1) To change area measurements
from m^2 to cm^2 multiply the
area in m^2 by 10 000
(e.g. $3\,m^2 = 30\,000\,cm^2$).

2) To change area measurements
from cm^2 to m^2 divide the
area in cm^2 by 10 000
(e.g. $45\,000\,cm^2 = 4.5\,m^2$).

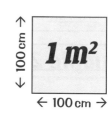

← 100 cm →
↑ 100 cm ↓
1 m²

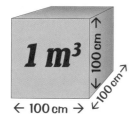

1 m³
↑ 100 cm ↓
← 100 cm →

> $1\,m^3 = 100\,cm \times 100\,cm \times 100\,cm = 1\,000\,000\,cm^3$

1) To change volume measurements
from m^3 to cm^3 multiply the
volume in m^3 by 1 000 000
(e.g. $3\,m^3 = 3\,000\,000\,cm^3$).

2) To change volume measurements
from cm^3 to m^3 divide the volume
in cm^3 by 1 000 000
(e.g. $4\,500\,000\,cm^3 = 4.5\,m^3$).

Remember: 1 ml is the same as a cubic centimetre. ➡ $1\,ml = 1\,cm \times 1\,cm \times 1\,cm = 1\,cm^3$

Swiss rolls and pi — a tasty little page...

You know the drill, learn this page. Learn it good. Only then my friend do you get to answer these:
1) Work out the surface area of a cylindrical drink can of height 12.5 cm and diameter 7.2 cm.
2) Convert these area measurements: a) $23\ m^2 \rightarrow cm^2$ b) $34500\ cm^2 \rightarrow m^2$
3) Convert these volume measurements: a) $5.2\,m^3 \rightarrow cm^3$ b) $100\,000\ cm^3 \rightarrow m^3$

Maps and Scales

If maps were the same size as the place they were showing, then they'd be big... and a bit pointless. Thankfully maps are usually made using <u>scales</u>. The most usual map scale is '<u>1 cm = so many km</u>'. This just tells you <u>how many km in real life</u> it is for <u>1 cm measured on the actual map itself</u>.

1) <u>Converting 'cm on the Map' into 'Real km'</u>

This map shows the original Roman M6 Motorway built by the Emperor Hadrian in the year AD120.

> The scale of the map is '1 cm to 8 km'
> "Work out the length of the section of M6 between Wigan and Preston."

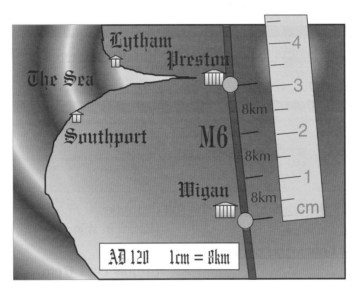

<u>This is what you do</u> (as shown on the diagram)

> 1) <u>PUT YOUR RULER AGAINST THE THING</u> you're finding the length of
> 2) <u>MARK OFF EACH WHOLE CM AND WRITE IN THE DISTANCE IN KM</u> next to each one
> 3) <u>ADD UP ALL THE KM DISTANCES TO FIND THE WHOLE LENGTH</u> of the road in km. (I.e. 8 km + 8 km + 8 km = <u>24 km</u>)

Of course if they just <u>tell you</u> the thing is, say, 5 cm long you won't be able to put your ruler on it. For example, they could say "The distance between Wigan and Southport <u>on the map</u> is 5 cm. How far is it in <u>real life</u>?"

In that case you should <u>draw a line</u> 5 cm long and <u>then mark off the km</u> on it <u>using your ruler</u> just the same:

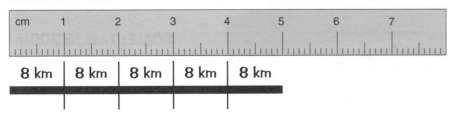

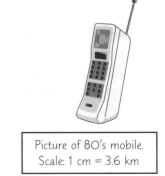

Picture of 80's mobile.
Scale: 1 cm = 3.6 km

So 5 cm on the map = 8 + 8 + 8 + 8 + 8 = <u>40 km</u>.

Maps and Scales

2) Converting 'Real km' into 'cm on the Map'

Example:

> "A map is drawn on a scale of 1 cm to 2 km.
> If a road is 12 km long in real life,
> how long will it be in cm on the map?"

Answer:

1) Start by drawing the road as a straight line:

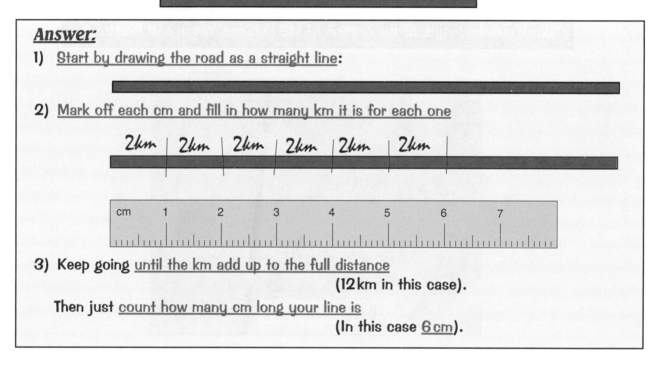

2) Mark off each cm and fill in how many km it is for each one

2km | 2km | 2km | 2km | 2km | 2km

cm   1   2   3   4   5   6   7

3) Keep going until the km add up to the full distance
   (12 km in this case).

Then just count how many cm long your line is
   (In this case 6 cm).

Instead of a map, you might get a question about a plan in your exam — like a plan of someone's bedroom or a garden. You do them in just the same way — the only difference is that the scale will probably be in m rather than km, e.g. 1 cm to 2 m. You might even be asked to draw something on a plan — just use the method above to work out how big it should be on the plan, then draw it.

What's a Roman soldier's favourite meal? Caesar salad...

If you're asked a map question in your exam — just remember the 3 steps for working with map scales. A ruler will be handy too. You're allowed to take them into exams. No need to hide one up your sleeve.

1) Work out the length in m of the runway shown here:

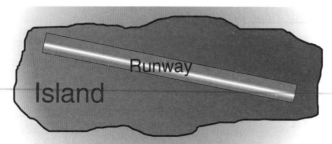

SCALE: 1 cm to 200 m

2) How many cm long would a 500 m runway be?

Compass Directions and Bearings

You probably already know what the <u>compass</u> is and how it can be really <u>useful</u>. By the end of this page you should have got your bearings about what is meant by <u>bearings</u> too. Ahem.

The Eight Points Of the Compass

Make sure you know all these <u>8 DIRECTIONS ON THE COMPASS</u>.

For <u>other directions</u> (i.e. not exactly North or South or South-East, etc), you have to use <u>BEARINGS</u>.

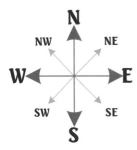

Bearings

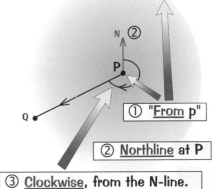

The bearing of A from B

1) A bearing is just a <u>DIRECTION</u> given as an <u>ANGLE</u> in degrees.

2) All bearings are measured <u>CLOCKWISE</u> from the <u>NORTHLINE</u>.

3) All bearings are given as 3 figures: e.g. 060° rather than just 60°, 020° rather than 20° etc.

The 3 Key Words

Only learn this if you want to get bearings <u>RIGHT</u>

1) 'FROM' Find the word '<u>FROM</u>' in the question, and put your pencil on the diagram at the point you are going '<u>from</u>'.

2) NORTHLINE At the point you are going '<u>FROM</u>', draw in a <u>NORTHLINE</u>.

3) CLOCKWISE Now draw in the angle <u>CLOCKWISE</u> from the <u>northline</u> to the line joining the two points. This angle is the <u>BEARING</u>.

EXAMPLE 1: Find the bearing of Q from P:

① "From p"

② Northline at P

③ Clockwise, from the N-line.

This angle is the <u>bearing of Q from P</u> and is <u>245°</u>.

EXAMPLE 2: The bearing of B from A is 060°. What is the bearing of A from B?

You need to use the angle laws you learnt in Unit 2 (see p66-67).

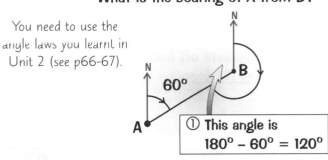

① This angle is 180° − 60° = 120°

② Angles around a point = 360°. So the bearing of A from B is 360° − 120° = <u>240°</u>

Compasses — we'd be lost without them...

Right, last page in the section. Just a few questions to go. Make sure you can draw out the <u>eight points</u> of a compass, and that you know the <u>3 key words</u> for bearings too. And you'll be reet petite.

1) Draw a blob on a piece of paper to represent home, and then draw <u>2 lines</u>, one going out in a <u>South-Westerly direction</u> and the other <u>on a bearing of 080°</u>.

Revision Summary for Unit 3 — Part 2

Only 12 questions stand between you and finishing GCSE maths revision... hurray!
<u>WHAT YOU'RE SUPPOSED TO DO HERE</u> is to put your Unit 3 constructing,
converting, calculating and drawing skills to the test.

1) Construct a triangle ABC with sides AB = 9 cm, AC = 10 cm and BC = 8 cm.

2) What is a locus? Describe in detail the four types you should know.
Also, draw a 60° angle and a 90° angle using the proper methods.

3) Draw the bisector of your 60° angle to make a 30° angle.

4) A plate has a <u>radius of 6 cm</u>. Find its <u>CIRCUMFERENCE</u>.

5) Delene wants to varnish the top of her new <u>circular</u> dining room table.
The table has a <u>radius of 1.25 m</u>. <u>One tin</u> of varnish will cover <u>2 m²</u>.
How many tins of varnish must Delene buy?

6) A car has a wheel of <u>radius</u> 0.5 m. How many times will
it need to rotate for the car to move forward 150 m?

7) A confectionery company is designing the packaging for a new brand of biscuits.
The packaging will be cylindrical, with a diameter of 4 cm and a height of 15 cm.
Calculate the surface area of the packaging.

8) Convert: a) 250 000 cm² to m²
             b) 2.1 m³ to cm³

9) Bobby is planning the layout of a new car park for his local supermarket,
shown below. Draw a plan of the car park using a scale of 1 cm to 5 m.

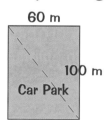

60 m

100 m

Car Park

10) Draw a diagram showing the <u>eight points</u> of the compass.

11) A ship sets off from Port P on a <u>bearing of 160°</u>.
<u>Show its direction</u> on the drawing below:

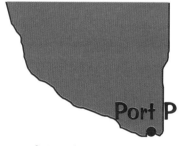

Port P

12) Another ship sets off on a <u>bearing of 240°</u>.
Show its direction on the drawing too.

Answers

Unit 1

P.4 Fractions, Decimals and Percentages: 1) a) 6/10 = 3/5 **b)** 2/100 = 1/50 **c)** 77/100
d) 555/1000 = 111/200 **e)** 56/10 = 28/5 or $5\frac{3}{5}$

P.5 Percentages: 1) £120

P.6 Ratio: 1) 56p **2)** £1000 : £1400

P.7 Ratio: 1) 1.5 kg **2)** £3500 : £2100 : £2800

P.8 Best Buys: Large size is best value at 1.90 g per penny.

P.9 Probability: 1) a) 1/13 **b)** 6/13 **c)** 3/26

P.10 Probability: 1) 1/5 or 20% or 0.2

P.11 Probability — Relative Frequency: 1) Landing on red: 0.43, landing on blue: 0.24, landing on green: 0.33

P.12 Data: 1) a) discrete **b)** qualitative **c)** qualitative **d)** continuous

P.13 Data: No, because it is only sampling one school year and music tastes might be different in different year groups.

P.14 Data: 1) a) This question is ambiguous. "A lot of television" can mean different things to different people.
b) This is a leading question, inviting the person to agree. **c)** The answers to this question do not cover all possible options.

P.15 Mean, Median, Mode and Range: First, order the data: -14, -12, -5, -5, 0, 1, 3, 6, 7, 8, 10, 14, 18, 23, 25
Mean = 5.27, Median = 6,   Mode = -5,   Range = 39

P.18 Averages and Grouped Data: (See table to the right.)

Length L (cm)	15.5 ≤ L < 16.5	16.5 ≤ L < 17.5	17.5 ≤ L < 18.5	18.5 ≤ L < 19.5	Totals
Frequency	12	18	23	8	61
Mid-Interval Value	16	17	18	19	—
Freq × MIV	192	306	414	152	1064

1) Mean = 17.4 cm
2) Modal class and median class = 17.5 ≤ L < 18.5

P.20 Tables, Charts and Graphs:

1) 0 | 3 6 7
    1 | 1 2 3 4 6 7 9
    2 | 0 2 4 6 6

2) Median = 16,   Range = 23

P.22 Bar Charts and Comparing Data: 1) See bar chart.

P.23 Pie Charts: See pie chart to the right.

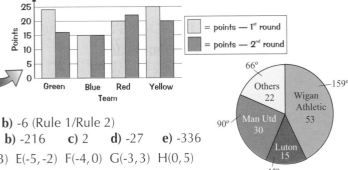

P.25 Negative Numbers and Letters: 1) a) +12 (Rule 1)   **b)** -6 (Rule 1/Rule 2)
c) x (Rule 2, then Rule 1) **d)** -3 (Rule 1)   **2) a)** +18   **b)** -216   **c)** 2   **d)** -27   **e)** -336

P.26 X and Y Coordinates: A(4, 5) B(6, 0) C(5, -5) D(0, -3) E(-5, -2) F(-4, 0) G(-3, 3) H(0, 5)

P.28 Straight-Line Graphs — Gradients: Gradient = -1.5

P.29 Real-life Graphs: Approx. 5 pints

P.31 Rounding Off: 1) a) 3.2 **b)** 1.8 **c)** 2.3 **d)** 0.5 **e)** 9.8

P.32 Rounding Off: 1) a) 3 **b)** 5 **c)** 2 **d)** 7 **e)** 3   **2) a)** 350 **b)** 500 **c)** 12.4 **d)** 0.036
3) a) 2900 **b)** 500 **c)** 100

P.35 Conversion Factors and Metric Units: 1) 160 kg **2)** 20 pints

P.37 Drawing and Measuring: 1) 1.5 m

P.38 Clock Time Questions: 1) 5:15pm **2)** 4:05pm **3)** 1,440 ; 86,400 **4)** 3hrs 30 min; 5hrs 45 min

Revision Summary for Unit 1 — Part 1

1) 4/5 **2)** 645/1000 = 129/200 **3)** £55.25 **4)** 240 **5)** £1.41 **6)** Biggest is best buy at 4.8 g per penny **7) a)** 53.3%
b) Add one more black ball, or take away one red or one green ball. **8)** H-1, H-2, H-3, H-4, H-5, H-6, T-1, T-2, T-3,
T-4, T-5, T-6 1/12 **9)** 0.8 **10)** Any three from: make sure your question is relevant; make your question clear, brief
and easy to understand; allow for all possible answers; make sure your question isn't leading or biased; make sure
your question isn't ambiguous; consider using grouped answers for a sensitive question like age. **11)** First put in order:
2, 3, 4, 6, 7, 7, 12, 15 **a)** 7 **b)** 6.5 **c)** 7 **d)** 13 **12)** Values of w from 50 to 60 **including** 50, but **not including** 60.
60 would go in the next group up. **13)** Mean ≈ ((75 × 15) + (105 × 60) + (135 × 351) + (165 × 285) + (195 × 206) +
(225 × 83)) ÷ 1000 = 160 680 ÷ 1000 = <u>161 min</u> **14) a)** Both things increase or decrease together and they're closely
related. (The more cheese you eat, the more you tend to have nightmares.)

Answers

b) No, the graph shows very weak correlation.

15) a) Angles are: Blue 108°, Red 135°, Yellow 36°, White 81°.

b) See pie chart.

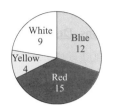

Revision Summary for Unit 1 — Part 2

1) a) +6 **b)** –32 **c)** –3 **d)** +5 **2) a)** It's a hit, so yes, he's cheating. **b)** Yes **3)** See right.
4) a) yes **b)** no **c)** yes **d)** no **5)** Gradient = 3 **6)** 2 cm³ / min **7) a)** 1 **b)** 3 **c)** 16 **d)** 12
8) a) 250 **b)** 900 **9) a)** 2 **b)** 2 **c)** 1 **d)** 3 **e)** 2 **10)** 20 rolls **11)** 10 **12)** £20.63 **13)** 17 miles
14) 12:50 pm

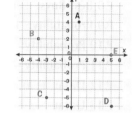

Unit 2

P.40 Ordering Numbers and Place Value:
1) a) One million, two hundred and thirty-four thousand, five hundred and thirty-one
   b) Twenty-three thousand, four hundred and fifty-six **c)** Two thousand, four hundred and fifteen
   d) Three thousand, four hundred and two **e)** Two hundred and three thousand, four hundred and twelve
2) 56,421 **3)** 9, 23, 87, 345, 493, 1029, 3004 **4)** 0.008, 0.09, 0.1, 0.2, 0.307, 0.37

P.41 Multiplying by 10, 100, etc: 1) a) 1230 **b)** 3450 **c)** 9650 **2 a)** 48 **b)** 450 **c)** 180 000

P.42 Dividing by 10, 100, etc: 1) a) 0.245 **b)** 6.542 **c)** 0.00308 **2 a)** 1.6 **b)** 12 **c)** 5

P.43 Addition and Subtraction: 1) a) 171 cm **b)** 19 cm **2)** 1.72 litres

P.45 Dividing Without a Calculator: 1) 336 **2)** 616 **3)** 832 **4)** 12 **5)** 121 **6)** 12 **7)** 179.2 **8)** 6.12 **9)** 56.1
10) 56 **11)** 30 **12)** 705

P.46 Prime Numbers: 1) 2, 3, 5, 7, 11, 13, 17, 19, 23, 29, 31, 37, 41, 43, 47   **2)** 97, 101, 103, 107, 109

P.47 Multiples, Factors and Prime Factors:
1) 7, 14, 21, 28, 35, 42, 49, 56, 63, 70 and 11, 22, 33, 44, 55, 66, 77, 88, 99, 110
2) 1, 2, 3, 4, 6, 9, 12, 18, 36 and 1, 2, 3, 4, 6, 7, 12, 14, 21, 28, 42, 84
3) a) 990 = 2 × 3 × 3 × 5 × 11 **b)** 160 = 2 × 2 × 2 × 2 × 2 × 5

P.48 LCM and HCF: 1) 8, 16, 24, 32, 40, 48, 56, 64, 72, 80 and 9, 18, 27, 36, 45, 54, 63, 72, 81, 90   LCM = 72
2) 1, 2, 4, 7, 8, 14, 28, 56 and 1, 2, 4, 8, 13, 26, 52, 104   HCF = 8   **3)** 63   **4)** 12

P.49 Powers: 1) a) 3^8 **b)** 4   **c)** 8^{12} **d)** 1   **e)** 7^6 **2) a)** 5^{12} **b)** 36 or 6^2 **c)** 2^5

P.50 Square Roots and Cube Roots: 1) a) 9 (other value is -9)   **b)** 3   **2) a)** g = 6 or -6 **b)** b = 5 **c)** r = 3 or -3

P.51 Fractions: 1) a) 5/6   **b)** 2/3   **2)** 3/5, 2/3, 11/15   **3) a)** 220   **b)** £1.75

P.52 Fractions: 1) a) 5/32   **b)** 32/35   **c)** 23/20 = 1 3/20   **d)** 1/40   **e)** 167/27 = 6 5/27

P.53 Fractions and Recurring Decimals: 1) 142857/999999   **2) a)** Terminating   **b)** Recurring   **c)** Terminating

P.54 Algebra: 1) a) 4x + y – 4   **b)** 9x + 5xy – 5   **c)** $5x + 3x^2 + 5y^2$ **d)** 6y – 4xy
2) a) 2x – 4   **b)** $5x + x^2$ **c)** $y^2 + xy$ **d)** 6xy – 18y

P.55 Algebra: 1) a) 5x(y + 3)   **b)** a(5 – 7b)   **c)** 6y(2x + 1 – 6y)   **2)** a = 156

P.56 Making Formulas from Words: 1) y = 5x – 3 **2)** C = 95n

P.57 Special Number Sequences: 1) EVENS: 2, 4, 6, 8, 10, 12, 14, 16, 18, 20, 22, 24, 26, 28, 30
ODDS: 1, 3, 5, 7, 9, 11, 13, 15, 17, 19, 21, 23, 25, 27, 29
SQUARES: 1, 4, 9, 16, 25, 36, 49, 64, 81, 100, 121, 144, 169, 196, 225
CUBES: 1, 8, 27, 64, 125, 216, 343, 512, 729, 1000, 1331, 1728, 2197, 2744, 3375
POWERS OF 2: 2, 4, 8, 16, 32, 64, 128, 256, 512, 1024, 2048, 4096, 8192, 16384, 32768;
POWERS OF 10: 10, 100, 1000, 10 000, 100 000, 1 000 000, 10 000 000, 100 000 000,
1 000 000 000, 10 000 000 000, 100 000 000 000, 1 000 000 000 000, 10 000 000 000 000,
100 000 000 000 000, 1 000 000 000 000 000 hmm...
2) a) 56, 134, 156, 36, 64   **b)** 23, 45, 81, 25, 97, 125   **c)** 81, 25, 36, 64   **d)** 125, 64   **e)** 64

P.59 Number Patterns and Sequences: 1) a) 20, 27 "Add one extra each time"   **b)** 2000 20 000 "Multiply the previous term by 10"   **c)** 4, 2 "Divide the previous term by 2"   **2)** 2n + 5

P.60 Midpoint of a Line Segment: 1) (3, 5)   **2)** (5, 1)

Answers

P.61 Drawing Straight-Line Graphs: **1)** and **2)**

x	-4	-2	-1	0	1	2	4
y	-6	-4	-3	-2	-1	0	2

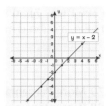

P.62 Straight-Line Graphs — y = mx + c:

1) 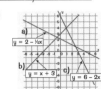   **2)**   **3)** -3

P.63 More Graphs: **1)** It means you're travelling back again.   **2)** Yes.

P.65 Angles: **1)** Actual angles given — accept answers within 10°: **a)** 36°   **b)** 79°   **c)** 162°   **d)** 287°

P.67 Parallel Lines: See right:

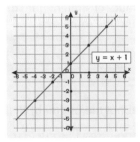

P.71 Symmetry:

H : 2 lines of symmetry, Rot^n symmetry Order 2,
T : 1 line of symmetry, No Rotational symmetry,
E : 1 line of symmetry, No Rotational symmetry,
S : 0 lines of symmetry, Rot^n symmetry Order 2

Z : 0 lines of symmetry, Rot^n symmetry Order 2,
N : 0 lines of symmetry, Rot^n symmetry Order 2,
X : 4 lines of symmetry, Rot^n symmetry Order 4,

P.72 Perimeters: **2)** 42 cm

P.74 Areas: **1)** 12 cm^2 **2)** 12 m^2 **3)** 21 m^2 **4)** 78 cm^2

P.75 Volume and Surface Area: V = 148.5 cm^3

P.76 Imperial Units: **1)** 1.5   **2)** 3 feet 10 inches   **3) a)** 200 or 220 yards   **b)** 187.5 cm

Revision Summary for Unit 2 — Part 1

1) Twenty-one million, three hundred and six thousand, five hundred and fifteen.   **2) a)** 2, 23, 45, 123, 132, 789, 2200, 6534 **b)** -7, -6, -2, 0, 4, 5, 8, 10   **3)** £120   **4)** 32p   **5)** 0.148 kg   **6) a)** 1456 **b)** 319 **c)** 88.2 **d)** 12
7) Prime numbers are: 2, 3, 7, 17, 19, 61   **8) a)** 6, 12, 18, 24, 30, 36, 42, 48, 54, 60   **b)** 1, 2, 4, 17, 34, 68   **c)** 2 × 2 × 2 × 5 × 7   **9)** 90   **10)** 24   **11) a)** 1296   **b)** 16 807   **c)** 16   **d)** 248 832   **e)** 2 048 000   **f)** 512
12) a) +16, –16 **b)** 6   **13) a)** $2\frac{14}{15}$ **b)** $1\frac{9}{16}$ **c)** $2\frac{7}{8}$ **d)** 11/21   **14) a)** Terminating   **b)** Terminating   **c)** Recurring
d) Recurring   **15)** 5x   **16) a)** 12g + 20h – 4   **b)** x^2 – 6x   **17)** 2x(1 + 3y)   **18)** y = 2x + 4   **19) a)** 19, 23; add 4 to the previous term   **b)** 6, 3; subtract one less each time   **20)** nth number = 4n – 3   **21)** midpoint = (-1, 2)
22) See table and graph below.   **23)** 6   **24)** How fast something is travelling.

x	-4	-2	0	2	4
y	-3	-1	1	3	5

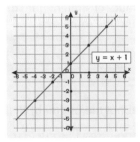

Revision Summary for Unit 2 — Part 2

1) See top of P.65   **2)** Yes (angle is about 45°)   **3)** Isosceles, X = 110°, Y = 40°   **4)** 50°

5) a)   **b)**   **c)**   **d)**

Answers

<u>6</u>) See P.69   <u>7</u>) **a)** A regular tetrahedron. **b)** A cuboid. **c)** A triangular prism.   <u>8</u>) 252°   <u>9</u>) 28 m   <u>10</u>) £1008
<u>11</u>) E.g. a cuboid measuring 3 cm by 2 cm by 5 cm   <u>12</u>) 17 miles   <u>13</u>) 65.45 kg   <u>14</u>) 1:15 pm

<u>Unit 3</u>

<u>P.79 More Percentages</u>: **1)** 30%
<u>P.80 Percentage and Reciprocals</u>: **1)** £70.50
<u>P.81 Solving Equations</u>: **1)** $x = 8$ **2)** $x = 7$
<u>P.82 Solving Equations</u>: **1) a)** $x = 4$ **b)** $q = 32$ **c)** $y = -2$ **2)** $b = \frac{1}{2}a + 3$
<u>P.83 Trial and Improvement</u>: $x = 1.6$
<u>P.84 Inequalities</u>: **1)** $x \geqslant -2$ **2)** $x \geqslant -4$, $x < 2$, $x = -4, -3, -2, -1, 0, 1$
<u>P.85 Quadratic Graphs</u>: See graph to the right.
Using graph, solutions are $x = -2$ and $x = 3$

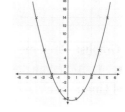

<u>P.86 Regular Polygons</u>:
1) A regular polygon is a many-sided shape where all the sides and angles are the same
2) Equilateral triangle, square, regular pentagon, regular hexagon, regular heptagon, regular octagon
3) Ext. angle = 72°, Int. angle = 108°   **4)** Ext. angle = 30°, Int. angle = 150°   **5)** See P.86

<u>P.87 Congruence and Tessellation</u>: **1)** i and ii are congruent.

<u>P.88 Pythagoras' Theorem</u>: **1)** BC = 8 m,
2) 5 m, 12 m, 13 m is a right angled triangle because $a^2 + b^2 = h^2$ works.
<u>P.91 The Four Transformations</u>:   A → B   Rotation 90° (¼ turn) clockwise about the origin.
B → C reflection in the line y = x.   C → A reflection in the y-axis.   A → D translation of 9 left and 7 down $\begin{pmatrix} -9 \\ -7 \end{pmatrix}$.
<u>P.93 Enlargements</u>:   **1)** 2430 cm² **2)** 1875 cm³

<u>P.94 Combinations of Transformations</u>: **1)**   **C→D**, Reflection in the y-axis, and an enlargement SF 2,
centre the origin, **D→C**, Reflection in the y-axis, and an enlargement SF ½, centre the origin.
2) **A'→B**, Rotation of 180° clockwise or anticlockwise about the point (0,3).

<u>P.99 Circles — Area and Circumference</u>: **1)** Area = 154 cm², circumference = 44 cm   **2)** 38 complete turns

<u>P.100 More Area and Volume</u>: **1)** 364 cm²   **2) a)**   230,000 cm² **b)** 3.45 m²
3) a) 5,200,000 cm³ **b)** 0.1 m³

<u>P.102 Maps and Scales</u>: **1)** 1400 m   **2)** 2½ cm

<u>P.103 Compass Directions and Bearings</u>: **3)** See right.

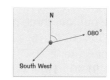

<u>Revision Summary for Unit 3 — Part 1</u>

<u>1</u>) 50p   <u>2</u>) £58.75   <u>3</u>) No, it would cost £36   <u>4</u>) **a)** 1/6   **b)** 1/12   **c)** 2   <u>5</u>) **a)** $x = 2$ **b)** $x = 3$ **c)** $x = -7$
<u>6</u>) **a)** $y = 6 - x$ **b)** $y = (x - 11) / 2$ **c)** $y = 3(7x + 3)$ or $y = 21x + 9$ <u>7</u>) $x = 5.5$ to 1 d.p.   <u>8</u>) **a)** $x < 5$ **b)** $x < -1$
c) $x > -5$ **d)** $x > 10$ <u>9</u>) **a)** straight line **b)** quadratic **c)** straight line **d)** quadratic   <u>10</u>) 45° and 135°
<u>11</u>) Congruence means having the same shape and the same size.
<u>12</u>) 4.72 m

<u>13</u>) **a)**   **b)**   **c)**

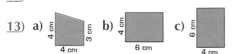
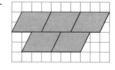

<u>14</u>) See p89   <u>15</u>) **a)** 90° anticlockwise rotation about the origin **b)** Reflection in the line y = 1   <u>16</u>) 3

<u>Revision Summary for Unit 3 — Part 2</u>

<u>1</u>) Measure all sides to check it's right.   <u>2</u>) and <u>3</u>) See p97&98   <u>4</u>) 37.7 cm   <u>5</u>) 3   <u>6</u>) 47.7 turns   <u>7</u>) 213.628 cm²
<u>8</u>) **a)** 25 m² **b)** 2100000 cm³   <u>9</u>) Scale drawing should have the dimensions 12 cm × 20 cm   <u>10</u>) See p103
<u>11</u>) and <u>12</u>) See right

Index

2D shapes 68, 69
3D shapes 70, 89

A

accuracy 33
acute angles 65
adding fractions 52
addition and subtraction 43
algebra 25, 54, 84
alternate angles 67
am and pm 38
analysing decimals 80
angles 23, 37, 65, 66, 67
angles — acute 65
angles in a 4-sided shape 66
angles in a triangle 66
angles — obtuse 65
angles on a straight line 66
angles — reflex 65
angles — right 65
angles round a point 66
appropriate degree of accuracy 33
arcs 69
area 73, 74, 75, 93, 99, 100
area — enlargements 93
area of circles 99
average 15, 16, 17, 18, 60

B

bar charts 22
bar-line graph 22
bearings 103
biased data 14
big numbers 40
bodmas 2
brackets 3

C

calculating tips 2, 3
centre of enlargement 90, 92
charts 19
chords 69
circles 69, 97, 99
circumference 99
classes 13
comparing numbers 79
compass directions 103
compasses (pairs of) 69, 96, 97
composite bar charts 22
cones 70
congruence 87
constructing accurate 60° angles 98
constructing accurate 90° angles 98
constructing triangles 96
constructions 97, 98
continuous data 12
conversion factors 34, 35
conversion graphs 29
converting decimals to fractions 4
coordinates 26, 60
correlation 21

corresponding angles 67
cross-sectional area 75
cube 70
cube numbers 57
cube roots 50
cuboid 70, 75
curved line graphs 63
cylinders 70

D

data 12, 13, 14, 16
decimal places 31
decimals 4, 31, 43
decimals (adding and subtracting) 43
decimals (dividing and multiplying) 45
denominators 53
diameter 69
diamonds 68
discounts 5
discrete data 12
distance 63, 77
dividing by 10, 100, etc 42
dividing fractions 52
dividing whole numbers 45
dividing without a calculator 45
downhill lines 27
d.p. (decimal places) 31
drawing and measuring 36, 37
drawing angles 37
drawing straight-line graphs 61, 62

E

edges 75
enlargements 90, 92-94
equal probabilities 9
equations of straight-line graphs 62
equations 81, 82
equilateral triangles 68, 86
equivalent fractions 51
estimating the mean of grouped data 18
estimating angles 65
estimating calculations 33
even numbers 57
exterior angles 66, 86

F

faces 75
factorising 55
factors 47, 48
factor tree 47
FDP method 79
finding the nth number 59
formulas 56
formula triangles 77, 93
four-sided shapes 68
fraction calculations 52
fractions 3, 4, 23, 51, 53
frequency 16, 18, 19, 22
frequency polygons 19
Froggatt's Lumpy Sprout Ketchup 35
Froggatt's "Slugtail Soup" 8

front elevation 89

G

giant sea-slug called Kevin 34
golden rules 6, 8
gradients 28, 30, 62
graphs 19, 27, 29, 61, 63, 85

H

HCF 48
heptagons 86
hexagons 86
highest common factor (HCF) 48
horizontal line 27

I

imperial units 76
improper fractions 52
increase (percentage) 5
inequalities 84
inequality symbols 84
interest 5
interior angles 86
intervals 17
isometric grids 70
isosceles trapezium 68
isosceles triangles 66, 68, 86

K

kites 68

L

LCM 48
letters 25
line graphs 19
line of best fit 21
line segment 60
lines of symmetry 68, 71, 90
loci 97, 98
lower bounds 36
lowest common multiple (LCM) 48

M

main diagonals 27
making formulas 56
maps and scales 101, 102
maximum values 36
mean 15, 16, 18
meaning of the gradient 30
measuring 36, 37
median 15, 18
memory buttons 3
metric-imperial conversions 76
metric units 34, 35, 76
mid-interval value 17, 19
midpoints 60
minimum values 36
mirror lines 91
mixed numbers 52
modal class/group 18
mode 15, 16

Index

multiple bar charts 22
multiples 47
multiplying by 10, 100, etc 41
multiplying decimals 44
multiplying fractions 52
multiplying letters 25
multiplying out brackets 54
multiplying whole numbers 44, 45
multiplying without a calculator 44

N

negative correlation 21
negative gradients 28
negative numbers 25, 84
nets 89
northlines 103
number lines 84
number patterns/sequences 57-59

O

obtuse angles 65
octagons 86
odd numbers 57
ordering fractions 51
ordering numbers 40
orientation 91
original value 79

P

parallel lines 67
parallelogram 68
pentagons 86
percentages 4, 5, 79, 80
perimeters 72
perpendicular 98
perpendicular lines 67
pi 88
pictograms 20
pie charts 23
plans 89
plotting points 61
p.m. 38
polygons 86
populations 13
porridge 7
positive correlation 21
positive gradients 28
powers 49, 57
primary data 12
prime factors 47, 53
prime numbers 46, 47
prisms 75
probabilities 9, 10, 11
probability scale 9
profit 79
projections 89
proportional division 7
proportions 4, 22
protractors 37
pyramids 70
Pythagoras' theorem 88

Q

quadrants 26
quadratic equations 85
quadratic graphs 85
quadrilaterals 68
qualitative data 12
quantitative data 12
questionnaires 14

R

radius 69
range 15, 16
ratios 6-8
rearranging formulas 82
reciprocals 80
rectangles 68, 73
rectangular tetrahedron 70
recurring decimals 4, 53
reduction (percentage) 5, 79
reflections 71, 91, 94
reflex angles 65
regular polygons 86
rhombus 68
right-angled triangles 68, 88
right angles 65
rotation 91
rotational symmetry 68, 71
rounding off 31, 32, 36
rounding whole numbers 32

S

sample space diagrams 10
sampling 13
scale factors 92, 93
scales (maps) 101, 102
scatter graphs 21
secondary data 12
sectors 69
segments 69
sequences 57, 58, 59
s.f. 32
side elevation 89
significant figures 32, 33
similarity 70
simplifying algebraic expressions 54
sloping lines through the origin 27
solids 70
solving equations 81, 82
speed 77
sphere 70
square-based pyramids 70
square numbers 57
square roots 50
squares 68, 86
stem and leaf diagrams 20
straight-line equations 27
straight-line graphs 27, 61, 62
subtracting fractions 52
subtraction 43
supplementary angles 67

T

surface area 75, 100
survey questions 13
symmetry 68, 71, 86

T

tables 19
tangents 69
terminating decimals 53
terms 54
Terry 90
tessellation 87
tetrahedrons 70
three letter angle notation 65
three-sided shapes 68
throwing a dice 9
time 38, 63, 77
tossing a coin 9
tracing paper 71
transformations 90, 91, 94
translations 90, 94
trapeziums 68
travel graphs 63
trial and improvement 81, 83
triangle construction 96
triangles 68, 96
triangular prisms 70, 89

U

unequal probabilities 10
uphill lines 27
upper bounds 36

V

VAT 5, 80
vectors 90
vertical lines 27
viewpoints 89
volumes 75, 100
volumes of enlargements 93

X

x-coordinates 26

Y

y-coordinates 26
y = mx + c 62